Intermediate Excel 2024

EXCEL 2024 ESSENTIALS - BOOK 2

M.L. HUMPHREY

SELECT TITLES BY M.L. HUMPHREY

EXCEL 2024 ESSENTIALS
Excel 2024 for Beginners
Intermediate Excel 2024
Excel 2024 Useful Functions

EXCEL 365 ESSENTIALS
Excel 365 for Beginners
Intermediate Excel 365
102 Useful Excel 365 Functions

EXCEL ESSENTIALS 2019
Excel 2019 Beginner
Excel 2019 Intermediate
Excel 2019 Formulas & Functions

EXCEL ESSENTIALS
Excel for Beginners
Intermediate Excel
50 Useful Excel Functions
50 More Excel Functions

WORD ESSENTIALS
Word for Beginners
Intermediate Word

POWERPOINT ESSENTIALS
PowerPoint for Beginners
Intermediate PowerPoint

ACCESS ESSENTIALS
Access for Beginners
Intermediate Access

See mlhumphrey.com for all titles by M.L. Humphrey

CONTENTS

CONTENTS (CONT.)

Introduction

In *Excel 2024 for Beginners*, we covered the basics you need to know to work in Excel on a daily basis, but Excel is an incredibly powerful tool that can do so much more than that.

So here we're going to continue from that solid foundation and cover some intermediate-level topics.

A lot of this will be more advanced tools for data analysis such as pivot tables (officially PivotTables), which let you take a table of data and quickly build a summary table of that data, charts, which let you visual your data, and conditional formatting, which lets you flag the results that meet your criteria.

If you don't use Excel for data analysis, we'll also cover topics such as converting text to columns, removing duplicate values, grouping and subtotaling data, and how to zoom your view in and out. (I use zoom more than ever these days thanks to video calls.)

I also want to revisit a few topics from the beginner book and dive deeper on them. So we'll discuss more advanced Find options, also cover Replace, circle back to the format painter, and cover how to sort horizontally.

The one big remaining intermediate-level topic we aren't covering here is formulas and functions in Excel. That has its own book, *Excel 2024 Useful Functions*.

Finally, I print these books in black and white to make them as affordable for readers as possible, but sometimes it is nice to see color images. The ebook versions of these books are in color and if you go to the About the Author section at the end of this book there is a discount code for buying the ebook off of my Payhip store.

But for now, let's just dive in and get started, shall we?

Basic Terminology Revisited

This chapter is for those who skipped *Excel 2024 for Beginners* or just want a quick refresh on the terminology I'll be using throughout this book.

Workbook

A workbook is basically an Excel file.

Worksheet

Workbooks are made up of worksheets, which according to Microsoft, are "the primary document that you use in Excel to store and work with data." They consist of "cells that are organized into columns and rows".

Another way to think of a worksheet is as a discrete location in your workbook that contains information.

Column

A standard worksheet uses columns and rows to create cells which display your information. Columns run across the top of the worksheet and are, by default, indicated with a letter.

Row

Rows run down the side of a worksheet and are numbered from 1 up to the very last row.

The number of columns and rows in a worksheet are fixed. When you insert or delete cells, columns, or rows you're actually moving information around, not changing the number of columns or rows in the worksheet.

Cell

Cells are formed by the intersection of a column and a row. They are referred to based upon the column and row where they are located. So the first cell in a worksheet is Cell A1, where A is the first column and 1 is the first row.

Click

If I tell you to click on something, that means to use your mouse (or trackpad) to move the arrow or cursor on the screen to a specific location, and then left-click or right-click as needed.

Left-Click/Right-Click

If you use a standard mouse then it's going to be split in the middle with the option to press down on either side at the front. Press on the left side and that's a left-click. Press on the right side and that's a right-click.

In general, a left-click will select an item, and a right-click will create a dropdown list of options to choose from.

If I don't tell you which one to use, left-click.

Left-Click and Drag

I may at times tell you to left-click and drag something. To do so, left-click on that object or in that location, and then hold your left-click as you move your arrow/mouse/cursor to either select a range or to move an object to its new location.

Formula Bar

The formula bar is the long white bar at the top of the screen with the function(x) (fx) symbol next to it. It shows the true contents of your cell, so, for example, the formula rather than the result of the formula.

Tab

I refer to the menu choices at the top of the screen (File, Home, Insert, Page Layout, Formulas, Data, Review, View, Help, etc.) as tabs. Each one will give you different tasks you can perform.

I may sometimes also refer to these as part of the menu at the top of the screen.

Section

I refer to the different named areas under each tab as a section.

Data

I use the terms data and information interchangeably. Whatever information you have in your worksheet is your data.

Table

I will sometimes refer to a table of data or data table. This is just a collection of cells that contain related information. Excel does now have a defined table functionality, but that is not what I'm referring to.

Scroll Bar

When there is more information than Excel can show you in a dropdown or worksheet, it will make scroll bars available on the right side or bottom of that space so you can "scroll" to see the rest of the information.

Select

When I tell you to select something, that means to click on it, or to choose a range of cells.

Dropdown Menu

A dropdown menu shows a list of potential choices that you can select from that aren't immediately visible. In the set of menu options up top, the existence of a dropdown menu is indicated by an arrow next to the current choice.

You can also right-click on various spots within Excel to see various dropdown menus. Right click on a cell or range of selected cell(s) to see the main dropdown menu in Excel.

Dialogue Box

Dialogue boxes are pop-up boxes that appear on top of your workspace. They contain options you can choose from to perform a task. They are generally there for older functionality, and often contain the largest number of choices.

Expansion Arrow

Some of the sections of the menu tabs have what I refer to as expansion arrows. These are arrows in the bottom right corner of that section which you can click on to open either a dialogue box or a task pane that contains more choices.

Task Pane

Task panes are separate spaces that sometimes appear to the left, right, or bottom of the worksheet area. They allow you to perform various tasks.

The easiest one to see is the Clipboard task pane which will open if you click on the expansion arrow in the Clipboard section of the Home tab.

To close a task pane, click on the X in the top right corner.

Cursor

Your cursor is what moves around when you move your mouse. Depending on where you are, it will look like different things. Often in Excel it looks like a variety of arrows. I may sometimes refer to moving your mouse around. This just means to move the cursor on the screen using the mouse or trackpad.

Arrow

If I ever tell you to arrow to something, that just means to use the arrow keys to navigate to that spot.

Control Shortcut

There are various keyboard combinations that you can use in Excel to perform common tasks. I refer to them as control shortcuts, because most use the Ctrl key, although not all of them do.

For example, Ctrl + C lets you copy your selection.

I write them with capital letters, but you don't need to use a capital of any of the letters, just hold down the keys at the same time.

Some Quick Tips

There were a few items I considered covering in *Excel 2024 for Beginners* but decided to move here instead, so let's cover those quickly.

Move to the End of a Data Range

When you have a table of data in your worksheet, you can use Ctrl + an arrow key to go to the last populated cell in that row or column in the direction of the arrow.

Watch out for gaps in your data, because it will stop just before the next empty cell.

To avoid stopping at each empty cell in a row or column, try starting in the first row or column of your data table. Assuming your table uses header rows or columns, or the first row or column are fully populated, that should work.

If there is no data in the worksheet, then Ctrl + an arrow key moves to the ends of the sheet.

Select an Entire Data Table

If you ever need to select all of your data in a data table, start in one corner of the table, and then use Shift + Ctrl + the arrow keys.

This will also stop at any blank cells, so you may need to use it more than once to capture all of the cells in the table.

Excel Appearance

The biggest impact on how Excel looks for you is likely going to be driven by your screen size. The smaller the screen as perceived by Excel, the less text you'll see for each menu tab. Excel reduces the different tasks down to their icons. You'll need to hold your mouse over each one to see what it does.

For example, I see this in the Data tab when at full-screen:

Here is that same section of the Data tab when I've reduced Excel to take up about a third of the screen:

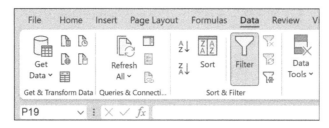

Note how all of the Get & Transform Data options no longer have labels. And the entire Data Tools section is now a dropdown menu.

* * *

Excel and Windows also have different display settings that can drastically impact the default appearance of Excel. The Office Theme settings can be accessed through the choices available in the bottom left corner of the Welcome Screen.

Either click on Account and use the Office Theme dropdown on the Account screen, or click on Options to bring up the Excel Options dialogue box. In the General section of that dialogue box, go to Personalize Your Copy of Microsoft Office, and change the Theme there.

The choices you have in Excel are Dark Gray, Black, White, and Colorful. You can also choose Use System Setting which will use your Windows settings.

I personally use Colorful. White will look much the same.

Sort Horizontal

In *Excel 2024 for Beginners,* we covered how to sort data. Usually you're going to sort results from top to bottom within a column or columns, but occasionally you may want to sort left to right within a row. For example, I once sorted a data table that counted concerns people had raised by most common concern to least common.

To sort horizontally, select your data, and then click on your preferred Sort option to bring up the Sort dialogue box. In the Sort dialogue box, click on Options in the top row.

That will bring up the Sort Options dialogue box:

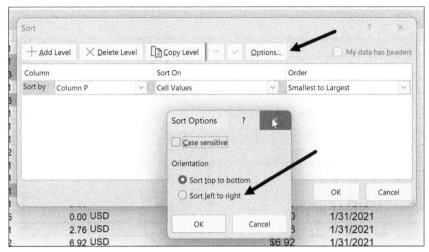

Click on the button for Sort Left to Right, and then click OK to go back to the main Sort dialogue box. Your Sort By option will change to a listing of the rows in your selected data instead of the columns. You can then proceed like a normal sort.

Custom Sort

If you have a text field that shows the day of the week or the month, choose the Custom List option under Order in the Sort dialogue box to find a list to sort that in the correct order:

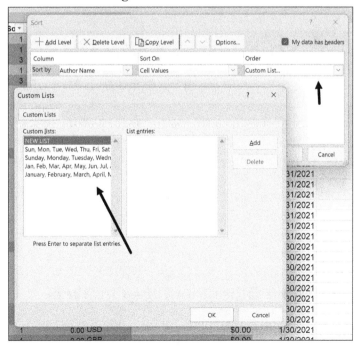

Excel has pre-populated custom lists for both the long and short versions of day of the week and month to choose from. Click on the one you want, and then on OK.

There is also an option there to create your own custom sort list. Choose the NEW LIST option on the left, and click on Add. That will let you enter values in the List Entries field. Type in your list with Enter after each value, and then click on OK.

The Order for that field will then show as your custom list:

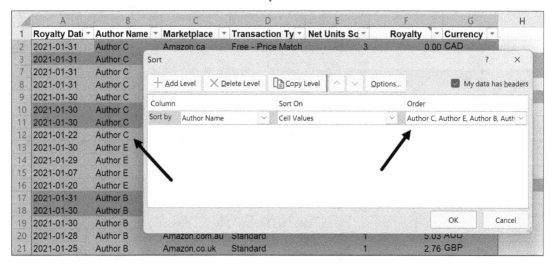

When you click OK the data will then sort in that order. (I sorted the data and then reopened my sort to show you the result and the sort entry at the same time.)

Select Multiple Worksheets

It is possible to have more than one worksheet selected by using Ctrl, and then clicking on multiple worksheet name tabs, or by clicking on your first worksheet name tab, using Shift, and clicking on your last worksheet name tab to select a range of worksheets.

If you do select multiple worksheets, be very, very careful, because if you type something into Cell A3 on your currently-visible worksheet while you have multiple worksheets selected, you will edit Cell A3 on *all* of the selected worksheets. I've used that to my advantage a few times, but more often I've messed up worksheets I didn't realize I was editing.

To unselect multiple worksheets, click onto the name tab for a worksheet you didn't have selected already, or right-click on a name tab for a selected worksheet, and choose Ungroup Sheets.

Open Other File Types In Excel

By default, when you try to open a file from Excel, your choices are going to be All Excel Files.

But there are some files that you can open from Excel that are not considered Excel Files. For example, Apple sends me sales data in .txt files that can be opened by a program like Excel, but aren't considered Excel Files.

To open a file like that, you have to Open the file from within Excel. Click on Open from the Welcome screen, then click on Browse to bring up the Open dialogue box. Change the file type dropdown to All Files, and navigate to where the file is saved.

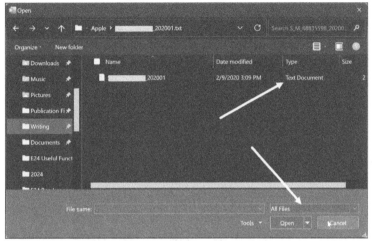

Click on the file name, and choose Open, like you would with any normal Excel file.

For text files, you may need to walk through the Text Import Wizard.

Most of the files like this will be Delimited, so you can just choose Next on the first screen. On the second screen, look in the Data Preview tab to make sure that the right character is selected as your delimiter.

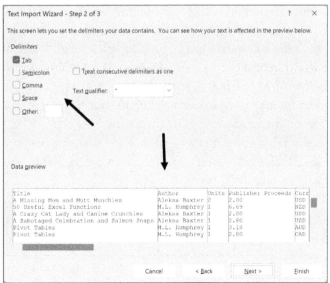

The delimiter is a character that separates columns of data and is deleted during import. Often it's a tab, a solid vertical line, a comma, or comma and space.

If the delimiter is not the correct one, type the correct character into the Other box, or check a different choice in that list.

If you want to work with a file like this that you imported, and keep the changes you make, be sure to Save As and choose a regular Excel file type before you close.

Excel Templates

On the Welcome Screen in Excel, as well as the New screen available under the File tab, you will see that Excel offers templates you can use.

These are pre-formatted Excel files that you can then add data to. I found a useful one that created timelines once by using the search online option. But to effectively use that template, I had to basically deconstruct how it worked. (In that case, the entries in the table had to be sorted in date order or the lines and data on the timeline didn't match.)

So these can be useful, but don't think that they'll necessarily do all the work for you.

To use one, just select it. But be sure to Save As with your file name when you're done.

Reformat a Date Column

It's ironic that while Excel, tries to turn anything close to a date into a date, it also seems to have an issue seeing some date values as dates when it comes to more complex analysis. I run into this with pivot tables and filtering, for example, on a regular basis. Even when a field is formatted as a date, Excel will still treat it as text.

To fix that (sometimes), you can select the column with your dates in it, go to the Data Tools section of the Data tab, and click on Text to Columns.

A Convert Text to Columns Wizard dialogue box will appear. Click Next on the first and second screens. On the third screen, choose Date as the column data format, and choose **DMY** from the dropdown menu. Click Finish.

The date in that column may not look any different, but Excel may now view those values as dates for things like filtering and pivot table timelines.

I say may, because while I was writing this book, I did that, it worked great, and then when I went back to do edits, it suddenly wasn't working. Same data. Same spreadsheet. Nothing I tried fixed it. So sometimes it really is them not you.

Another option if that doesn't work, may be to use the DATEVALUE function to create dates from text entries. They'll come out as the numeric equivalent of a date, so you'll then need to format the entries to a date format, but that's another option.

I also sometimes use the DATE function paired with RIGHT, LEFT, and MID to rebuild a date from a text entry. That one is also hit or miss.

File Naming

If I am going to have a lot of files in a folder that I need to be able to quickly access, like monthly bank statements, I will include at the beginning of the file name the date of the document in YYYYMMDD order. That's year-month-date. The reason to do that is so your files will automatically be in date order, even if one of them is edited at some later point in time.

Please, never, ever name your files using something like 3.30.24. It seems fine, right? But if you have files across multiple years it puts the month files together instead of the year files together. So you have all of March together instead of all of 2024 sorted by month.

Trust me, this matters when you have a lot of records to deal with.

Also, I'm pretty sure that the period in that format interferes with searching your file names. So no periods in a file name either.

You can put the date at the end if you want, but only do that if the rest of the file name is going to be the same. So I could have different versions of this file and name them something like "Excel 2024 for Beginners 20241001" and then "Excel 2024 for Beginners 20241005".

Same goes with using V1, V2, etc. for versioning. Think about how the file names will be listed if you alphabetize them, and name accordingly. Better to use V1 through V23 instead of Final, Final V2, Final Final, etc.

Find and Replace

In *Excel 2024 for Beginners* I briefly touched upon a basic search which can be done by using Ctrl + F to bring up the Find and Replace dialogue box. Now it's time to revisit Find and also discuss Replace.

The control shortcut for Find is Ctrl + F, the control shortcut for Replace is Ctrl + H. They both will open the Find and Replace dialogue box, the only difference is which tab it opens to. In the Editing section of the Home tab you can also use the Find & Select dropdown menu to choose either Find or Replace to also open the Find and Replace dialogue box.

Let's start with Find:

Find

Narrow Results Using Match Case

By default, if I type "sec" into the Find What field, Excel's Find will look for "sec" in any part of any cell. It will return entries for secretive, section, securities, Securities, SEC, etc

But often I want to narrow the search results down to something more specific, like SEC, which in my day job is the abbreviation for the Securities and Exchange Commission.

To narrow your results based on the capitalization of the word, click on Options in the basic Find dialogue box.

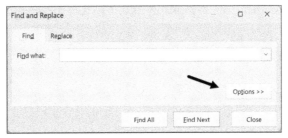

This will expand the dialogue box and show more search options. Check the box for Match Case to limit your search result to only those entries that have the exact same capitalization as your search term:

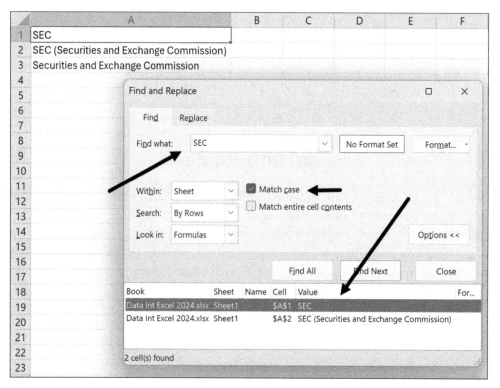

Here you can see that I had three entries that used the letters "sec", but only two that used the capitalized "SEC" that I searched for. By clicking on Match Case, Excel only returned those two results.

Narrow Results to Match Entire Cell Contents

Unfortunately, Excel does not have an option to search for a whole word only like Word does. But it does have the ability to search for only the cells that contain your specified text.

To do that, click on the Match Entire Cell Contents checkbox. Here I've kept Match Case checked and also checked that box to limit my result to just the result that has "SEC" in a cell and nothing else:

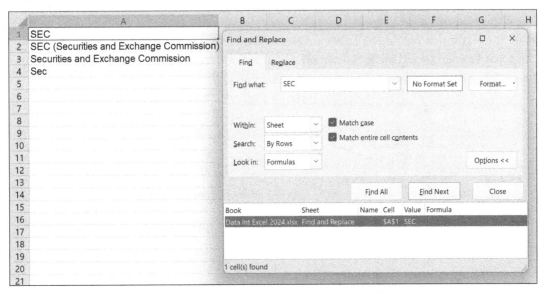

Limit Search By Selecting Cells

Another quick little trick with Find in Excel is to select only some of the cells in a worksheet. That will limit your search to just those cells. I often use this when the data I'm looking for is limited to one column, like customer name.

(This is something to keep in mind in the opposite direction, too. Sometimes you'll tell Excel to search for something you know exists and it won't give you a result. If that happens, check that you don't have some cells selected already that are limiting it to searching in just those selected cells.)

Expand Search Results to Entire Workbook

By default, Excel will only search in your current worksheet. But under the expanded options section you can change the Within dropdown from Sheet to Workbook to look in all of the worksheets in your workbook at once.

Include Formula Results in Search

A normal Excel search looks at the text in your formulas or cells, but not the results of any formulas. Change the Look In dropdown from Formulas to search your visible cell contents.

(That dropdown also allows looking in Notes or Comments if you have those in your workbook.)

Search by Format

If you click on Format on the right-hand side of where you enter the text you want to search for, you can specify an exact format to search for.

In Word I do this a lot to look for italics in my documents. I leave the Find What field blank and set it to italics and it finds all italicized text in my entire document for me.

When you click on that, it will open the Find Format dialogue box. Just choose your formats from each tab like you would in the Format Cells dialogue box.

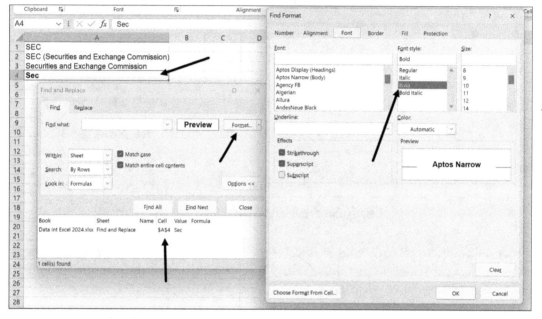

Here you can see that it searched for bolded text for me based on my choice in the Find Format dialogue box. That Preview text in the Find dialogue box shows a sample of the format I told it to search for.

A Caution When Using Find

Be careful once you've used Find after opening Excel, because the Find function in Office tends to default to whatever your last settings were on your last search.

So especially if you use any of the special options to search for something, you need to clear them out if you want to go back to using a basic search. (This happens in Word, too.)

Good news is it resets back to baseline if you close and reopen the program. Not ideal, but if your search just isn't behaving the way you think it should, this is sometimes easier than trying to figure out what setting you need to fix to bring it back to normal.

Replace

Replace lets you find something and also replace it with something else. It's a wonderful, glorious, highly dangerous tool to use.

Here is what the Replace tab of the Find and Replace dialogue box looks like:

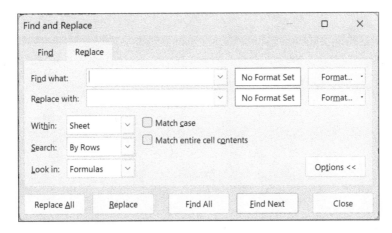

At it's most basic, it's very easy to use. You type what you want to find into the first field, Find What, and then you type what you want to replace it with into the Replace With field.

The problem comes when someone thinks, "Let me replace SEC with Securities and Exchange Commission" and then uses default find parameters. They then end up with "Securities and Exchange Commissionurities and Exchange Commission" where they used to have "Securities and Exchange Commission".

Excel is a tool that only works as well as the user who tells it what to do. And replace is one of those areas where unexpected errors often occur.

To help prevent issues, you can use Find All to see which fields will get changed before you make any replacements.

Or you can use Find Next to go to the next cell where a replacement will be made and only click on Replace if you're sure you want to change that value.

I would also recommend using all of the tricks we discussed above with Find to control your results.

Only use Replace All with extreme caution. And if you do use it, be sure to look through your results before you move on. Replace is one of those areas in Excel where you can irretrievably break your data if you're not careful.

For example, let's say I wasn't careful in our example above, and replaced "SEC" with "Securities and Exchange Commission" in my worksheet without any find constraints. I was then in a hurry to get to lunch and closed and saved without checking the result.

You can't just reverse "Securities and Exchange Commission (Securities and Exchange Commissionurities and Exchange Commission)" by using Replace again. You'd end up with "SEC (SECurities and Exchange Commission)".

Now, that's a pretty obvious error to spot and correct. Where it gets really painful is someone replacing "he" with "she" or something basic like that where maybe some entries already were she and become sshe, or where there were other words that used "he" like "hear" that become "shear". So ALWAYS check the results if you use Replace, and only use it with care.

Remove Duplicates

Remove Duplicates does exactly what it sounds like it does—it looks at your data and removes the duplicates, so that you're left with a list of only the unique values or combination of values.

I use Remove Duplicates all the time. It's an easy way to create a list of unique entries from a column of data. It can also remove duplicate rows of information if those exist in your data table.

Let's look at a couple examples.

Here is a single column of data that spans six hundred rows and has repeating values:

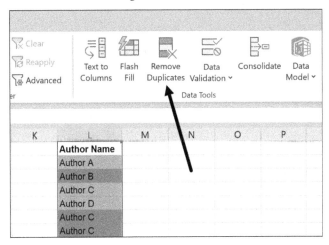

I want to know the unique author names in this column. I could apply the filter option to the column if I was just curious to see approximately how many there are, but if I need to use that list elsewhere, then Remove Duplicates is the way to get it.

To do this, select the column with your data, go to the Data Tools section of the Data tab, and click on the Remove Duplicates option. (It looks like three stacked cells with an X in the bottom right corner.) That will bring up the Remove Duplicates dialogue box:

It's very easy when you just have the one column of data. Check or uncheck the My Data Has Headers box at the top so Excel knows whether there's a header row or not, and then click OK.

If you tell Excel there's a header row, it will skip that first row. Otherwise, it will include that value when looking for duplicates.

You'll then see something like this where Excel tells you the number of duplicates removed and number of unique values remaining.

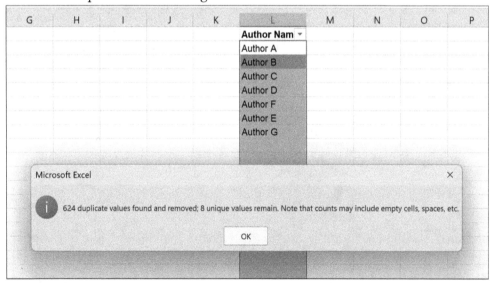

Note that the column I applied it to now has a very small number of unique results left. Ignore the number of unique values it tells you remain, though, since often one of the "unique values" that remains is a blank cell which you really don't want to count.

One thing to be careful of with Remove Duplicates, is that Excel is going to look at the entire contents of your cell to determine whether two cells are identical or not. I recently had a data set where things looked the same on the surface, but weren't. I had "State" in one field and what looked like "State" in another, but the second field had an extra space before the word in one cell and an extra two spaces after it in another. For the purpose of Remove Duplicates, those values were not the same.

So if you are removing duplicates from a very long list, I suggest sorting when you're done, and scanning down the list of values to make sure that you don't have multiples that snuck through because of something like that. (If you know how to use functions, the TRIM function can be applied first to a column of data to remove extra spaces at the start or end of the entries, which will cut down on issues like that.)

While I often use Remove Duplicates for a single column of data, it can also be used for multiple columns. When used that way, it looks for the unique combinations of values across all of the selected columns. That means you may have duplicates of a value in one column, but you won't have duplicates across the entire row.

See, for example, the image below, where you have Author E listed twice in Column E, once for when it occurs with Amazon.com and once for when it occurs with Amazon.it.

If the column(s) of values that you want to apply this to are part of a larger data table, I strongly recommend that you copy and paste the column(s) to a new worksheet first. That's because otherwise you can break your data.

Here is an example:

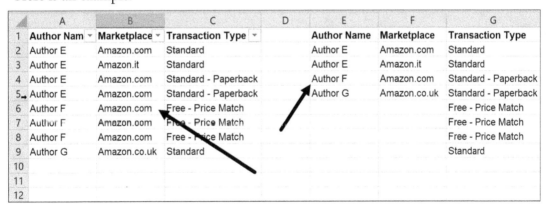

In Columns A through C you can see my original data. I copied that data to Columns E through G, selected just Columns E and F, and then removed duplicates.

You can see that after I did that, the values in Columns E and F no longer match to the values in Column G. See how Author F on amazon.com was a Free-Price Match transaction in the original data in Row 6? Now it's in Row 4 and looks like it was a paperback transaction.

This happens because when Excel removes duplicates, it just fills in each new unique combination in the next row available without any consideration for what data is around that.

Excel does sometimes prompt you to make sure you want to do that. Here it did so for a single column within a larger data table:

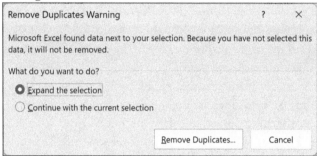

But not always. When I selected two columns from that table, it just went right ahead and removed duplicates without warning me.

This is why I recommend that if you're going to use Remove Duplicates on a data table, that you use it on all columns in that table, or copy the columns you're going to use to a new location first.

Hide or Unhide Columns or Rows

I often hide columns of information that I don't need to see when working with a larger worksheet. Especially if I'm inputting information into a worksheet where I need to enter that information in columns that aren't near each other, say Column B and Column F.

Rather than have to tab or arrow from Column B to Column F for every single row, it's far easier to just hide Columns C through E for a little bit. Another reason to do this is if you build a worksheet that contains columns for calculations that don't need to be visible to all users.

I sometimes will also hide rows of data that I've already verified, for example.

The first step is to select the column(s) or row(s) that you want to hide. Next, right-click and choose Hide from the dropdown menu.

Another option for hide and unhide is to go to the Cells section of the Home tab, and use the Format dropdown. The Visibility section of that dropdown has a secondary dropdown menu called Hide & Unhide that allow you to hide or unhide rows, columns, or sheets.

To unhide column(s) or row(s), though, I select the columns or rows on either side of the ones that were hidden, right-click, and choose Unhide from the dropdown:

If you have multiple sets of hidden columns, or multiple sets of hidden rows, and you want to unhide them all at once, you can click in the top left corner to Select All (or use Ctrl + A), and then right-click on any of the columns or rows in the worksheet, and choose Unhide.

But you can only unhide all columns or all rows at once, you can't do both at the same time.

Another option for hide and unhide is to go to the Cells section of the Home tab and use the Format dropdown. There is a Visibility section that has a secondary dropdown menu called Hide & Unhide.

* * *

One final thing to know about when you hide columns or rows, is that it's not as obvious as filtering. When you filter, the numbering of the rows changes color to let you know.

With Hide, that doesn't happen. Instead you'll just see a very faint double line where the columns or rows are hidden.

And, of course, the column letters or row numbers will also be missing.

Here, for example, I've hidden Columns D through F and Rows 4 through 6:

Group or Ungroup

There are certain situations where I want to hide column(s) or row(s), but I also want to be able to easily see them, too, as needed. In that case, using group is a better choice than hiding the columns.

For example, the other day I was gathering five years of annual performance data. I had data for each quarter, but I didn't need to see it, I just needed the year-end numbers.

I grouped the columns with the quarterly numbers so I could hide them, while also keeping them easily accessible in case my boss wanted to see the details.

Let's walk through an example. Here's my data:

	A	B	C	D	E	F	G	H
1		Q323	Q423	Q124	Q224	FY 23-24	Q324	Q424
2	Sales	$1,234.56	$2,354.87	$1,274.96	$4,213.25	**$9,077.64**	$1,237.96	$4,521.87
3	Costs	$ 235.79	$ 124.59	$ 546.28	$ 123.69	**$1,030.35**	$ 546.89	$ 364.57
4	Net	$ 998.77	$2,230.28	$ 728.68	$4,089.56	**$8,047.29**	$ 691.07	$4,157.30

I want Columns B through E grouped together. To do that, I can select all four columns, go to the Outline section of the Data tab, and click on Group.

Excel places a line above those columns with a minus sign at the end. Clicking on that minus sign hides those columns, and turns the minus sign into a plus sign.

To demonstrate both visible and hidden grouped columns, I went ahead and grouped Columns B through H, too:

	A	F	G	H	I	J
1		FY 23-24	Q324	Q424	Grand Total	
2	Sales	$ 9,077.64	$ 1,237.96	$ 4,521.87	$ 14,837.47	
3	Costs	$ 1,030.35	$ 546.89	$ 364.57	$ 1,941.81	

It's probably a little hard to see in the image above, because the Microsoft folks seem to be going for subtle these days as opposed to easy to see, but there is a line that stretches from where Column B would be to above Column I with a minus sign at the end.

There is also a + sign above Column F.

The minus sign indicates a group of columns that is currently expanded but can be collapsed. The plus sign indicates columns that are currently collapsed/hidden but can be expanded to be visible.

If I click on the minus sign, all of the columns under that line from Column B to Column H will be hidden. If I click on the plus sign over Column F, then the columns that are hidden there (which we know are Columns B through E) will reappear.

Note that there are also numbers on the left-hand side that correspond to each of those lines.

I can click on the 3 to expand all of the groups and make all columns visible, or click on the 1 or 2 to hide the columns in that group.

You may also note a double line between Columns A and F that indicates hidden columns.

To ungroup column(s) or row(s), expand the group, and then select the column(s) or row(s) you want to ungroup, go to the Outline section of the Data tab, and click on Ungroup. If you don't expand the group first, the minus sign along the perimeter will go away, but the column(s) or row(s) will remain hidden, so you'll then need to Unhide them.

If you don't select the grouped column(s) or row(s) first, nothing will be ungrouped when you choose Ungroup.

If you only select a subset of the grouped column(s) or row(s), only they will be ungrouped. Any existing group will be split into two groups on either side of the ungrouped columns or rows.

When columns or rows are grouped, using Tab, arrows keys or Enter will take you to the next visible cell, skipping over those hidden columns or rows.

Subtotals

When you apply Subtotals to a data table, Excel will perform a calculation on your designated fields after every change in the value of a different field. Sum of sales at each change in marketplace, for example.

You have to be careful with this one, though, because the data needs to be sorted properly or your results will be wonky. So, first things first, select the cells in your data table, and sort on the value you want to use. (Marketplace in this case.)

Once your data is sorted properly, go to the Outline section of the Data tab, and click on Subtotal.

This will bring up the Subtotal dialogue box:

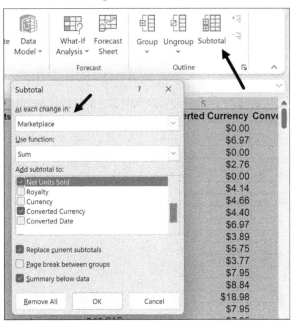

Change the first dropdown to choose the column you sorted on. At each change in the values in that chosen column, Excel will perform the designated calculation.

The next dropdown tells Excel what calculation to perform. The default is Sum, but you can also choose count, average, minimum, maximum, product (multiply all the values), count numbers only, standard deviation, and variance.

Finally, check the boxes next to the columns you want Excel to perform that calculation on. In this case, I want net units sold and converted currency.

Click OK.

Excel will look at the designated column, and each time the value in that column changes it will perform the specified calculation on the values in your chosen column(s).

Here's what I get:

	Royalty Date	Author Name	Marketplace	Transaction Type	Net Units Sold	Royalty	Currency	Converted Currency	Cor
1	Royalty Date	Author Name	Marketplace	Transaction Type	Net Units Sold	Royalty	Currency	Converted Currency	Cor
2	2021-01-31	Author C	Amazon.ca	Free - Price Match	3	0.00	CAD	$0.00	
3	2021-01-30	Author A	Amazon.ca	Standard	1	6.97	CAD	$6.97	
4	2021-01-31	Author C	Amazon.ca	Free - Price Match	65	0.00	USD	$0.00	
5	2021-01-31	Author D	Amazon.ca	Standard	1	2.76	USD	$2.76	
6	2021-01-31	Author C	Amazon.ca	Free - Price Match	1	0.00	EUR	$0.00	
7	2021-01-19	Author A	Amazon.ca	Standard	1	4.14	CAD	$4.14	
8	2021-01-19	Author A	Amazon.ca	Standard	1	4.66	CAD	$4.66	
9	2021-01-19	Author A	Amazon.ca	Standard	1	4.40	CAD	$4.40	
10	2021-01-18	Author A	Amazon.ca	Standard	1	6.97	CAD	$6.97	
11	2021-01-15	Author A	Amazon.ca	Standard	1	3.89	CAD	$3.89	
12	2021-01-14	Author A	Amazon.ca	Standard	1	5.75	CAD	$5.75	
13	2021-01-20	Author A	Amazon.ca	Standard - Paperba	1	3.77	CAD	$3.77	
14	2021-01-19	Author A	Amazon.ca	Standard - Paperba	1	7.95	CAD	$7.95	
15	2021-01-27	Author A	Amazon.ca	Standard - Paperba	1	8.84	CAD	$8.84	
16	2021-01-12	Author A	Amazon.ca	Standard - Paperba	1	18.98	CAD	$18.98	
17	2021-01-02	Author A	Amazon.ca	Standard - Paperba	1	7.95	CAD	$7.95	
18	2021-01-12	Author A	Amazon.ca	Standard - Paperba	1	7.95	CAD	$7.95	
19	2021-01-07	Author A	Amazon.ca	Standard - Paperba	1	7.95	CAD	$7.95	
20	2021-01-06	Author A	Amazon.ca	Standard - Paperba	1	7.95	CAD	$7.95	
21			Amazon.ca Total		85			$110.88	
22	2021-01-30	Author C	Amazon.co.uk	Free - Price Match	1	0.00	GBP	$0.00	
23	2021-01-31	Author A	Amazon.co.uk	Standard	1	2.72	GBP	$3.29	

You can see that Row 21 has total values for units sold and converted currency, and that all values for marketplace above that row are Amazon.ca.

By default, all rows of your data as well as the subtotals will be visible.

To collapse your results to just the subtotals, click on the 2 on the left-hand side of the row numbers. You'll then see something like this:

	Royalty Date	Author Name	Marketplace	Transaction Type	Net Units Sold	Royalty	Currency	Converted Currency	Converted Date
1	Royalty Date	Author Name	Marketplace	Transaction Type	Net Units Sold	Royalty	Currency	Converted Currency	Converted Date
21			Amazon.ca Total		85			$110.88	
120			Amazon.co.uk Total		105			$451.74	
620			Amazon.com Total		1,233			$6,176.81	
628			Amazon.com.au Total		7			$49.84	
630			Amazon.com.mx Total		1			$40.25	
632			Amazon.de Total		3			$0.00	
634			Amazon.es Total		1			$2.82	
636			Amazon.fr Total		1			$5.14	
638			Amazon.in Total		1			$0.00	
642			Amazon.it Total		3			$9.34	
643									
644			Grand Total		1440			6846.82	
645									
646									

I recommend always doing that and then scanning the list of bolded entries to make sure they're unique.

This is what that would've looked like if I didn't sort my data first:

			A	B	C	D	E	F
		1	Royalty Da ▾	Author Nam ▾	Marketplace ▾	Transaction ▾	Net Units S ▾	Royalty ▾
+		3			Amazon.com Total		1	
+		5			Amazon.com.au Total		1	
+		8			Amazon.com Total		66	
+		10			Amazon.fr Total		1	
+		12			Amazon.ca Total		3	
+		14			Amazon.com Total		1	
+		16			Amazon.de Total		3	
+		23			Amazon.com Total		7	
+		25			Amazon.co.uk Total		1	
+		34			Amazon.com Total		13	
+		36			Amazon.com.au Total		1	
+		42			Amazon.com Total		12	

The arrows on the left are pointing at multiple entries for Amazon.com. The arrows on the right are pointing at multiple entries for Amazon.com.au. Something we do not want.

This happens because Excel performs the specified calculation at *each* change in the values in the designated column. If you don't sort your data, Excel can end up creating multiple calculations for the same value.

Remember, Excel is a tool. And it is only as good as the user and the data it is given. Give it bad data, you will get bad results.

Okay, a few more things.

After you collapse your data to just the subtotal rows, you can click on any of the plus signs on the left-hand side to see the detail for that value, or you can click on the 3 to see all of the details again.

Also, the Subtotal dialogue box has a few extra options available at the bottom.

By default the box for Summary Below Data should be checked. That gives you a grand total row for all entries in your data. If you don't want that, uncheck it.

You can also check a box for Replace Current Subtotals to replace any subtotals you have with your new choices.

And if you want each group of results to be on its own page, you can check Page Break Between Groups.

To remove subtotals, I select my data table again, reopen the Subtotal dialogue box, and then click the Remove All option.

Finally, for the extra credit types, you may want to check out the Excel help for subtotals. It will show you how to create subtotals within subtotals. I'm not covering that here because I prefer to work in pivot tables for that sort of thing.

Pivot Tables - Basics

I wrote the first ever Excel Essentials series just so I could teach writers how to use pivot tables, that's how valuable I think they are.

At their most basic, pivot tables (technically spelled PivotTables by the Office folks) are a quick and easy way to take a big table of data and summarize it. You don't have to worry about how things are sorted or which order your columns are in or writing the correct formula, you can just throw it all in a pivot table and Excel will do the hard work for you.

But there is a lot to know to use them effectively.

Now. A few things to keep in mind:

Pre-Prep

You may need to do a little work with your data first to clean it up and standardize it. For example, Excel can't tell that CO and Colorado are the same thing, so will treat them as different values. You'll want to take a copy of your data and fix issues like that before you start using a pivot table to summarize your results.

You should also make sure that your columns are formatted properly so that numbers are seen by Excel as numbers and dates are seen as dates. (See the quick tips chapter for how to fix dates when working with pivot tables.)

Also, remove any subtotals or grand totals, and make sure that each column of your data has a header in the first row of the table. (For me, I prefer that this is also the first row of the worksheet.)

And make sure that each row of data is complete in and of itself. You want to be working with a table of data not data formatted as a report.

Dynamic Nature

Also, be careful where you choose to build a pivot table. Pivot tables are dynamic. The amount of space they take up varies depending on your data and the choices you make about what to include in the table.

If you put a pivot table in a worksheet that has other information, you run a risk that the pivot table will overwrite that other data.

Pivot tables build to the right and down, so if you do put a pivot table in a worksheet that has other information in it, always add that pivot table to the right of and/or below your existing information.

And if you are ever tempted to add notes around an existing pivot table (like I sometimes do), understand that if you update the table you could either accidentally delete your notes, or the data in your pivot table could move so that it no longer matches up with your notes.

(This is one reason why if you use a formula and try to reference values in a pivot table it looks so weird. Excel can't just reference a cell like with normal data entries, it has to instead reference how the value in that cell was built.)

Okay. Now that we've gotten through the preliminaries, let's build one.

Insert

Assuming your header row is in the first row of your worksheet, select the columns that have your data, or use Select All. If your data table doesn't start at the top of the worksheet, then select all of the cells in your table, being sure to include the header row.

Next, go to the Tables section of the Insert tab, and click on the PivotTable image.

If you accidentally click on the dropdown arrow, the option you want is From Table/ Range. (For the level of expertise I expect you to have if you're reading this book, I really do not recommend working with data in another workbook or from another source. It's too easy to break the link between your workbook and that external data source, so we're not going to go there.)

You should now see a PivotTable From Table or Range dialogue box:

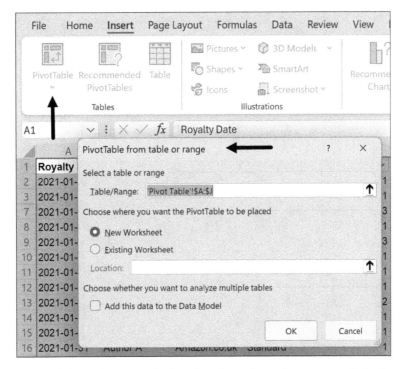

Usually, I just click OK here, because I already selected my data range, I don't work with data models, and I am fine with putting my pivot table in a new worksheet.

However, sometimes I do click on the option for Existing Worksheet instead, and then click somewhere to the right of the data in my current worksheet, to keep the data and the pivot table together in that same worksheet. I usually do that in workbooks where I have a lot of pivot tables I'm going to build to make sure I know the source of the data in each table.

At this point, you may see an error message if any of the cells in the first row of your selected data are blank. That's because Excel needs there to be something to label each column of data with.

If that happens, close out, and either add labels to the blank cells in the first row of your selected cell range, or delete any blank columns in your cell range.

If a blank column header isn't the issue, then you may need to fix your referenced cell range to make sure you captured the header row. Once you've fixed whatever the issue is, go through the above steps again.

By default, Excel will insert your pivot table starting in Cell A3 of a new worksheet:

There won't be an actual pivot table there, though, until you tell Excel which fields to use. It just shows you that it's ready to put a pivot table there.

You should also see a PivotTable Fields task pane on the right-hand side of the workspace, as well as two new menu tabs, PivotTable Analyze and Design:

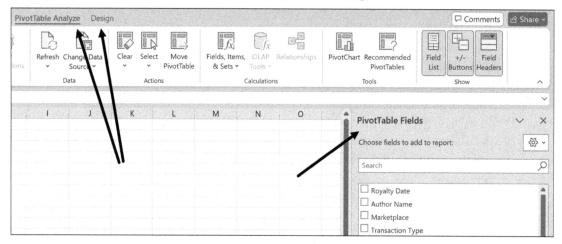

The task pane and tabs will be visible by default any time you're clicked onto a pivot table, but will go away when you click elsewhere in your worksheet or workbook. So to get them back if they ever disappear, just click onto your pivot table.

Build

The way you build a pivot table is by using the PivotTable Fields task pane on the right-hand side of the workspace.

Here is the full task pane:

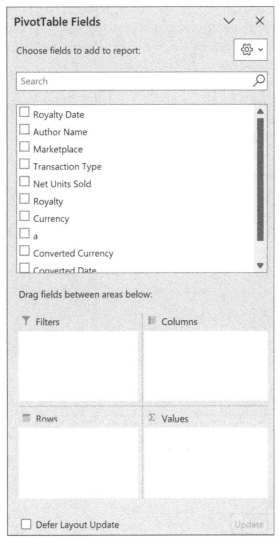

The top section shows all of your available fields. At the start, that will be the names for each column of data you included. (Later it might include extra date-related fields or formulas if you add any.)

The bottom section has four parts: Filters, Columns, Rows, and Values. This is where you put each field to build the table.

The fields you place in Columns and/or Rows will provide the data labels you'll have either across the top (columns) or down the side (rows) of the table. Values is where you put the field(s) you're going to use for calculations.

Filters is for fields you aren't going to use in your columns, rows, or values sections, that you still want to use to narrow down the information displayed in the pivot table.

Let's walk through some examples to see how this works. We're going to use the same data I've been using throughout these books, which contains about six hundred lines of book sales data that includes fields for date of sale, author name, marketplace, type of transaction, number of units sold, currency, royalty, and converted royalty.

First, let's build a table that shows units sold for each author.

My Values field, what I want to use for my calculation, is going to be Units Sold. And then either my Row or Column field needs to be Author Name.

To do this, I simply left-click and drag each of those fields from the top of the PivotTable Fields task pane down to the appropriate section in the bottom of the task pane. I went with the Row section for Author Name because it looked better to me:

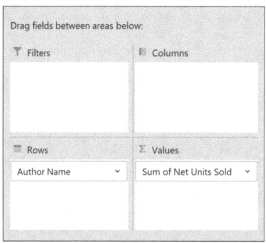

Another option for adding a field to a section, is to right-click on the field name in the top section, and then choose where to place the field from the dropdown menu:

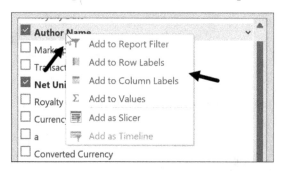

Either way works.

(In older versions of Excel you could also drag the field to the table in the worksheet, but that's no longer available by default. This is why it's always good to know at least two ways to do things in Excel. That way if they change one of the two, you can still use the other method.)

Okay.

Here is the pivot table that created:

	A	B	C
1			
2			
3	Row Labels ▾	Sum of Net Units Sold	
4	Author C	90	
5	Author E	4	
6	Author B	20	
7	Author A	1242	
8	Author D	80	
9	Author F	3	
10	Author G	1	
11	(blank)		
12	**Grand Total**	**1440**	
13			

Excel automatically built the table as I placed each field.

Now let's make this more complex and add in Marketplace. I want to see how many units each author sold in each marketplace.

I also want to be able to see total sales by marketplace and total sales by author, which means one has to be in the Rows section and one has to be in the Columns section, they can't be together.

Because it was easy, I added Marketplace into the Columns section:

This is what that pivot table looks like:

	A	B	C	D	E	F	G	H	I	J	K	L	M
1													
2													
3	Sum of Net Units Sold	Column Labels											
4	Row Labels	Amazon.ca	Amazon.co.uk	Amazon.com	Amazon.com.au	Amazon.com.mx	Amazon.de	Amazon.es	Amazon.fr	Amazon.in	Amazon.it	(blank)	Grand Total
5	Author A	15	90	1129	3	1		1	1		2		1242
6	Author B		10	7	3								20
7	Author C	3	1	81			3		1	1			90
8	Author D		3	76	1								80
9	Author E			3							1		4
10	Author F			3									3
11	Author G		1										1
12	(blank)												
13	Grand Total	18	105	1299	7	1	3	1	2	1	3		1440
14													

I can easily see how many units each author sold in each marketplace, as well as totals for each author and totals for each marketplace.

Not bad for clicking and dragging three field names into place, huh?

Filter Pivot Table Data

Now let's apply a filter. To do that, add the field you want to use as your filter to the Filters area of the PivotTable Fields task pane.

For this example, I used Transaction Type:

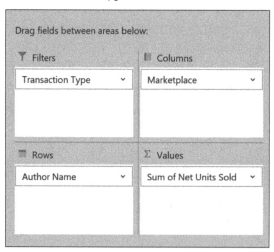

Doing that adds a dropdown menu above the pivot table that you can then use to change what information is displayed in the pivot table itself.

Here, for example, I limited the results to Free-Price Match. Now the pivot table only shows results for transactions that were free price match transactions:

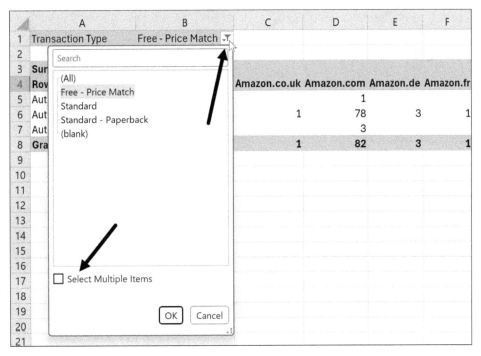

	A	B	C	D	E	F	G	H	I
1	Transaction Type	Free - Price Match							
2									
3	Sum of Net Units Sold	Column Labels							
4	Row Labels	Amazon.ca	Amazon.co.uk	Amazon.com	Amazon.de	Amazon.fr	Amazon.in	Grand Total	
5	Author B			1				1	
6	Author C	3	1	78	3	1	1	87	
7	Author F			3				3	
8	Grand Total	3	1	82	3	1	1	91	
9									

The filter dropdown works just like when you filter columns in a normal worksheet.

Click on the dropdown arrow or funnel on the right-hand edge of the cell (see below) that displays the current filter to see the dropdown.

Check the box for Select Multiple Items at the bottom of the dropdown so you can then check and uncheck the boxes to select the values you want to filter by. The default is All, so if you only want one or two values, uncheck that box for All to unselect all values first, and then check the ones you want.

You can also use the search field to narrow your results.

When you select a single value to filter by, like I did above, Excel will show that value, as you can see in Cell B1 of the pivot table we just built.

If you use multiple criteria, though, it will just say Multiple Items instead. In a situation like that, it may be better to use a Slicer, which is discussed in the next chapter.

Filter Values in Rows or Columns

There will be times when you want to use a field for your rows or columns sections, but you also want to limit which of those values display in the pivot table. You can't put that field in the Filters section, because you're using it in the Rows or Columns section already, and Excel won't let you do both.

Fortunately, you can still filter those values. Just click on the arrow next to Row Labels or Column Labels in your pivot table to bring up a filter dropdown menu for that field:

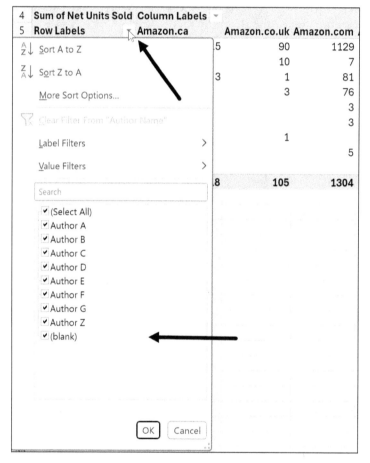

At that point it's just working with filters again.

If you have multiple fields in your rows or columns sections and want to filter on one of them, click on one of the values in the table for that field first, and *then* click on the arrow next to Row Labels or Column Labels.

Multiple Fields in a Section

You can use multiple fields in the Columns, Rows, Filters, and/or Values sections. To have multiple levels, just drag more than one field to that section.

For Columns and Rows, order matters. It's like with sorting. Put the field you want to be primary on top, and list secondary, tertiary, etc. fields below that in order of priority. Values for the primary field will only show up once. Values for the other fields can repeat.

Here, for example, I have a pivot table with Transaction Type in the first position and Author Name listed second:

4		Amazon.in
6	**Free - Price Match**	
7	Author C	1
8	Author F	
9	Author B	
10	**Standard**	
11	Author A	
12	Author D	
13	Author B	
14	Author C	
15	Author E	
16	Author G	
17	**Standard - Paperback**	
18	Author A	
19	Author D	
20	Author E	
21	Author B	
22	**Grand Total**	**1**

Note how you only see each transaction type listed once, but Author B is listed three times, once per transaction type.

For Values, the order just dictates which one will be displayed first in the table. Here I have Net Units Sold in the first position and Converted Currency in the second position:

	A	B	C
1			
2	Transaction Type	(Multiple Items)	
3			
4	**Row Labels**	**Sum of Net Units Sold**	**Sum of Converted Currency**
5	Author A	1242	$6,415.27
6	Author B	19	$59.52
7	Author C	3	$8.98
8	Author D	80	$305.28
9	Author E	4	$17.55
10	Author G	1	$0.42
11	(blank)	1440	
12	**Grand Total**	**2789**	**$6,807.02**
13			

For Filters the order doesn't matter.

One final note here. Be very careful if you have multiple fields in more than one section of your pivot table. It can be done, but it can also get really messy really fast. Always ask yourself if what you've done is the best way to present this information. Maybe two tables is a better choice.

Expand/Collapse Fields

When you have more than one field in a column or row in a pivot table, you can expand and collapse the levels to show or hide the detail below. This can be done one entry at a time, or across all entries at once.

It's easy enough to hide or show the detail for one particular entry, you just click on the plus or minus sign to the left of the label. Plus expands, minus collapses (hides).

Here I've put Author Name on top and Marketplace underneath in the Rows section, and then clicked on the negative sign next to Author A to collapse that detail.

3	Sum of Net Units Sold	Column Labels								
4		<12/10/2020	<12/10/2020 Total	2020	2020 Total	2021				2021 Total
5	Row Labels	<12/10/2020		Qtr4		Qtr1	Qtr2	Qtr3	Qtr4	
6	Author A			1	1	880	114	122	120	1236
7	Author B					17	3			20
8	Amazon.co.uk					10				10
9	Amazon.com					4	3			7
10	Amazon.com.au					3				3
11	Author C					90				90
12	Amazon.ca					3				3
13	Amazon.co.uk					1				1
14	Amazon.com					81				81
15	Amazon.de					3				3
16	Amazon.fr					1				1
17	Amazon.in					1				1
18	Author D			1	1	50	16	8	5	79
19	Amazon.co.uk					3				3
20	Amazon.com			1	1	46	16	8	5	75
21	Amazon.com.au					1				1

Author A now has a plus sign I can click if I want to expand that part of the table again. Authors B, C, and D still have a minus sign and show all of their related marketplace details.

To collapse or expand all entries for a specific level at once, right-click on one of the values (Author A, Author B, etc.), go to the Expand/Collapse option in the dropdown menu, and then use the secondary dropdown menu to make your choice.

For each level you have in a pivot table, the bottom of that dropdown will show an option to expand or collapse to that level:

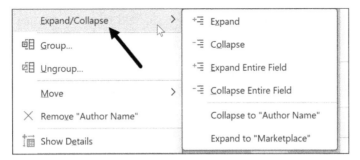

Expand Entire Field shows all of the detail for all values at that level in the table; Collapse Entire Field hides all the details for all values at that level.

Collapse and Expand just collapse or expand for that item at that level in the pivot table.

(I usually just end up playing around with the different choices when I need this rather than memorizing it.)

Remove a Field

The easiest way to remove a field that you were using to build your pivot table is to just uncheck the box next to its name in the PivotTable Fields task pane.

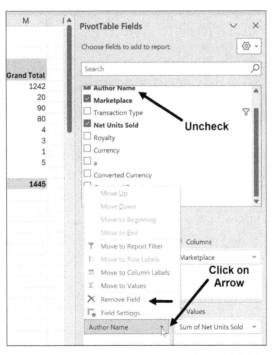

You can also left-click on the arrow next to the name of the field in the bottom section, and choose Remove from the dropdown menu.

This is the best approach if you were using that field more than once in the table (which we'll discuss later).

Another option is to right-click on a value in the pivot table itself, and then choose "Remove [Field Name]" from there.

If you were using that field as a filter, it is best to unfilter first before you remove the field, or the data in your table may remain filtered.

Move a Field

To move a field to a different section of your pivot table (Rows to Columns, Columns to Rows, Filters to Rows, etc.), you can left-click on the field name in the bottom section of the task pane and drag it to the section where you want it.

You can also left-click on the arrow for that field in the bottom section of the task pane to choose a new location from that dropdown menu.

Or you can right-click on the field name in the top of the task pane, and choose a location from that dropdown menu.

If you already had the field in a section, Excel will remove it from that prior section to place it in the new one.

(Also, note that Undo is a little tricky here. If you move a field, realize that was a mistake, and want to move it back, you will probably need to click into your worksheet first before Undo will work.)

Sort Results

You can sort the data in your pivot table. For example, I often want my largest values in my grand total column at the top.

To sort, right-click on a value in the column you want to sort by, go to the Sort option, and in the secondary dropdown menu choose the type of sort you want:

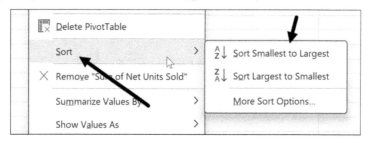

The nice thing about sorting in a pivot table is that all of your values stay together. You don't have to worry about breaking your data if you don't select the whole table first.

If you sort your column values, the sort will automatically be a left to right sort, but if you want a left to right sort for the calculated values in your table, you need to use More Sort Options in the Sort secondary dropdown. That will bring up the Sort by Value dialogue box, where you can then tell Excel you want a left to right sort:

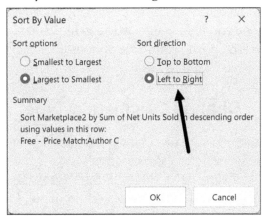

Move Column or Row Entries In the Pivot Table

You can also manually rearrange the column or row entries in your pivot table.

To do so, right-click on a value that you want to move, go down to the Move option, and then use the secondary dropdown menu to choose whether to move the value to the Beginning, the End, up one space, or down one space:

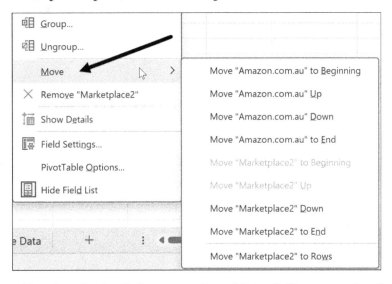

When working with values in the Columns section, think of Up as meaning "to the left" and Down as meaning "to the right".

It can help to think through the ultimate order you want your values in before you start doing this. For example, it's easier to move a field to the beginning and then down one, rather than move it up five times.

And sometimes you can save a lot of effort by moving your fields to the beginning or end in the order that puts the one you truly want at the end in that end position last.

We'll discuss a few more organizing your table options in the next chapter, but for now let's cover some more basics that you need to know.

Change Calculation Type

One of the issues I run into often with pivot tables and my data, is that Excel defaults to count when I drag my number fields into the Values section.

Fortunately, Excel will still sum those values if I ask it to, and it also does indicate what calculation it is performing on a field in the Value section of the PivotTable Fields task pane. (If you look above, you'll see that it was summing net units sold, for example.)

If you ever need to change the type of calculation, one option is to click on the dropdown arrow for that field in the Values section, and then choose Value Field Settings from the dropdown menu:

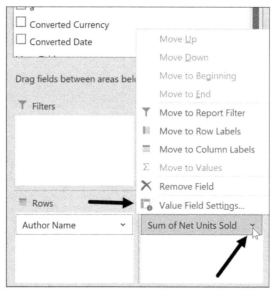

That will open the Value Field Settings dialogue box:

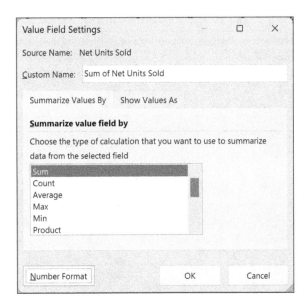

In the Summarize Value Field By section of the dialogue box, you will then see a list of the possible calculations that Excel can perform. It's the standard list of Sum, Count, Average, Max (maximum), Min (minimum), Product, Count Numbers, standard deviation, and variance that you will see throughout Excel. Just click on the option you want and then click OK. (I usually also format my cells at this point in time. We'll talk about that in a moment.)

When you change the calculation type, the Custom Name field will update accordingly.

Another way to choose the calculation type is to right-click on a calculated value in the pivot table itself, and then use the secondary dropdown menu for Summarize Values By:

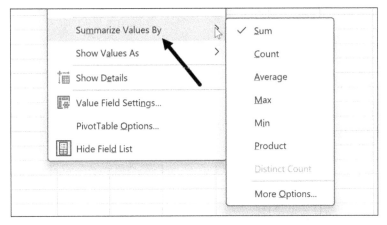

That approach doesn't require opening the dialogue box, so is pretty handy to use. It is a more limited list, but usually I just want Count or Sum, so it would work for me, I'm just used to the other way.

Excel also has a Show Values As option in that dropdown menu or as a tab in the Value Field Settings dialogue box:

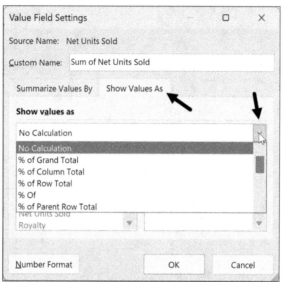

By default, that is going to show as No Calculation, which basically means it will display the result of the calculation you chose for Summarize Values By. (Sum, Count, etc.) But if you click on the dropdown arrow in the dialogue box, or use the secondary menu from the pivot table, you can choose to have Excel show your result as a percentage calculation, a difference from some value, a running total, a rank, or an index:

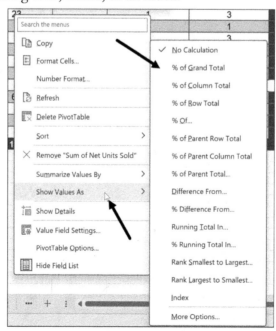

For example, I am sometimes not as interested in the number of units sold by an author in a marketplace as I am in what *percent* of sales that author represents in each marketplace. I have some marketplaces (the U.S.) with much larger absolute sales numbers, so sales in other markets (like France) look small in comparison no matter what. But it's valuable to know if Author A is 60% of sales in both of those markets or only one of them. That can help me make advertising decisions for each market.

The first step if you're going to do this, is to choose the correct calculation for Summarize Values By. (Sum or Count, usually.) After you do that, go to Show Values As, and pick the type of calculation you want displayed.

Here is that same data from our author and marketplace pivot table above, but now set to show the percentage of the column total instead of units:

	A	B	C	D	E	F	G	H
1								
2								
3								
4	Sum of Net Units Sold	Column Labels						
5	Row Labels	Amazon.ca	Amazon.co.uk	Amazon.com	Amazon.com.au	Amazon.com.mx	Amazon.de	Amazon.es
6	Author A	83.33%	85.71%	86.91%	42.86%	100.00%	0.00%	100.00%
7	Author B	0.00%	9.52%	0.54%	42.86%	0.00%	0.00%	0.00%
8	Author C	16.67%	0.95%	6.24%	0.00%	0.00%	100.00%	0.00%
9	Author D	0.00%	2.86%	5.85%	14.29%	0.00%	0.00%	0.00%
10	Author E	0.00%	0.00%	0.23%	0.00%	0.00%	0.00%	0.00%
11	Author F	0.00%	0.00%	0.23%	0.00%	0.00%	0.00%	0.00%
12	Author G	0.00%	0.95%	0.00%	0.00%	0.00%	0.00%	0.00%
13	(blank)	0.00%	0.00%	0.00%	0.00%	0.00%	0.00%	0.00%
14	Grand Total	100.00%	100.00%	100.00%	100.00%	100.00%	100.00%	100.00%

It's a little hard to read because of all of the 0.00% entries, but if you can wade through that, you can see that Author A tends to be the majority of sales in each marketplace, but is not in Australia (AU) and Germany (DE). That would be worth exploring more. (And we can fix that formatting to make this easier to read.)

Note that it is possible in the Values section to add the same field more than once. So you can, for example, show the sum or count value AND a % value.

Here, for example, I have actual number of units sold by author as well as the percent of the total:

	A	B	C
1			
2			
3	Row Labels	Units Sold	Percent of Units Sold
4	Author C	90	6.25%
5	Author E	4	0.28%
6	Author B	20	1.39%
7	Author A	1242	86.25%
8	Author D	80	5.56%
9	Author F	3	0.21%
10	Author G	1	0.07%
11	(blank)		0.00%
12	Grand Total	1440	100.00%
13			

(I took out marketplace because it would have been way too busy and also renamed the columns to something friendlier and formatted them to center the values.)

A Caution

If you ever build a pivot table that has more than one different field in the Values section, be careful about using different calculations for each column. If you put a column that has a count of values next to another that has a sum of values next to another that has an average, it is possible someone will mistake the type of calculation being performed in one of those columns. You can do it, no one will stop you, just step back and ask yourself how someone who didn't build the table and is maybe in a hurry is going to interpret it. This is when changing your column labels will really be useful.

Rename a Field

Speaking of. You can rename a field that you're using in your pivot table by clicking on the cell that has the field name in it and then changing the name in the formula bar. If you try to use the original field name, though, you will get an error message that the name already exists. So if I want to rename "Sum of Net Units Sold" which was built using the "Net Units Sold" field, I can use "Units Sold", no problem, but I can't use "Net Units Sold" again.

You can also change the name by going to the Active Field section of the PivotTable Analyze tab, but that takes more effort.

Format Values

Another issue I almost always encounter with pivot tables is that the numbers won't be formatted the way I want them to be. For example, my currency values never seem to be formatted as currency by default.

You can technically just select the visible cells in the table, go to the Home tab, and use the formatting options there like you would with any other cell in Excel, but I do not recommend that. Because the formatting you apply to those cells will not carry through if the table updates.

The better way to format your values is to use the Value Field Settings dialogue box. (Right click on the field name in the Values section and choose Value Field Settings from the dropdown to open it.)

From the dialogue box, click on the bottom left corner where it says Number Format. That will bring up the Format Cells dialogue box, where you can then choose the number format you want applied to that field. Click OK to close the Format Cells dialogue box, and then OK to close the Value Field Settings dialogue box when you're done.

Here, for example, I've changed the formatting of the percentage values to not have two decimal places, which makes it a little easier to read:

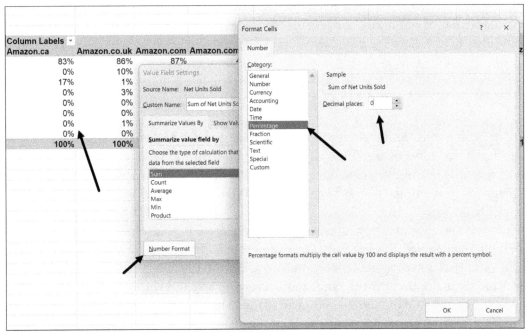

(I made the change and then reopened both dialogue boxes so you could see what each one looks like.)

Refresh Pivot Table

Your pivot table will not automatically recalculate everything when you add new data to the original data source. To update your table, go to the Data section of the PivotTable Analyze tab, and you'll see Refresh:

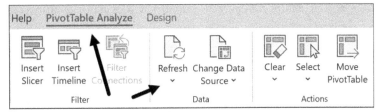

Click on the image there and your table should update to show your changes.

You can also choose Refresh All from the dropdown there, and that will update all pivot tables in the workbook.

There are control shortcuts for this, too, but I never use them. They are Alt + F5 and Ctrl + Alt + F5, respectively.

(One thing to be careful of with Refresh is that it can undo some of your custom formatting, so try to finalize your data before you get fancy with the formatting. Microsoft support seems to think that the PivotTable Options choices can fix this, but it didn't for me when I just tried it. Honestly, I normally don't need pretty formatting of my pivot tables because they're just there for my analysis and I take the results elsewhere if I need them for a report.)

Change Data Source

There are going to be times when you need to change the data that Excel is using for a pivot table. Maybe you add a new column of data that you want to use, or you were selecting a cell range for the table and have now added more rows of data that you need to capture. When that happens, you can go to the Data section of the PivotTable Analyze tab, and click on Change Data Source.

That will take you to the worksheet where the data is, and also bring up the Change PivotTable Data Source dialogue box. The easiest way, in my opinion, to change the data source is to just left-click and drag in the worksheet to select the full range of cells to use in the pivot table. That should update the cell range in the dialogue box and you can then just click on OK to close it. Your pivot table should automatically update based on your new cell range.

Another option is to click into the field in the dialogue box and manually adjust the range of cells being referenced. I do this when I add another column of data because I can just click at the end, backspace out the last listed column letter, and type in the new letter.

Just be careful with this approach, because using arrows to move within the text in that input field does not work well. (It will start populating a cell range for you in the midst of the one you already had.) If you go with this approach and are making significant changes, I think it's best to delete out what's there first, and then you can hold down Shift as you arrow around to select the new cell range.

If you don't want to do that, then click exactly where you need to make your edit in that field, and use backspace or delete before type in your values from there.

Just do not use the arrow keys.

A Quick Caution

One final note here about refresh, change data sources, and filtering. I've noticed lately that Excel is a little less stable when using these than it used to be. It sometimes doesn't update the values. So be sure to "gut check" that your table results look right. Maybe make sure the grand total is what you expect, or that all the values you should be seeing are there.

Do something to independently confirm your results if you're using refresh, change data sources, or filters.

There have been a couple times in Excel 365, where I have had to do a brand new pivot table to get it to work properly. Also, when I was playing around here with two fields in the Filter section and then removed them, one of the filters continued to apply to my table even though I'd supposedly taken it away. That's why I suggested unfiltering your table first.

Pivot tables are great and invaluable, so don't let that scare you away from using them. Just understand that for anything you do in Excel, you should always make sure the result makes sense.

Clear Your Pivot Table

If you ever build a pivot table and want to just start over from scratch, you can go to the Actions section of the PivotTable Analyze tab and choose Clear.

If you have filters in place on your table, you can use Clear Filters from the dropdown menu to reset those.

Pivot Tables – More Advanced Topics

The last chapter covered the basics of building a pivot table and editing it a bit. I'd say I can get away with only the information in that chapter for probably 90%-95% of what I do with pivot tables. (There are a few more items in the formatting chapter that I use regularly.) But there are a lot of bells and whistles with pivot tables, and they're adding more functionality all the time, so let's walk through some of those more advanced topics now.

Working with Dates

In more recent version of Excel, pivot tables have gotten really useful for working with dates. But only if Excel recognizes the field as a date field. Given Excel's tendency to turn anything remotely close to a date into a date, it is kind of ironic how difficult it can be sometimes to get Excel to treat an actual date as a date for pivot table purposes. (I put some tips at the start of this book, but sometimes even those don't work.)

Okay. So what can Excel do with dates?

When you add a date field to the Rows or Columns section of a pivot table, Excel will create up to four separate date fields for you in that section. You'll have the actual date field, but Excel will also create fields for year, quarter, and month based on your date values. (Assuming your dates span multiple months, quarters, and/or years.)

Here I dragged Royalty Date to the Columns section and you can see the new fields Excel created for me.

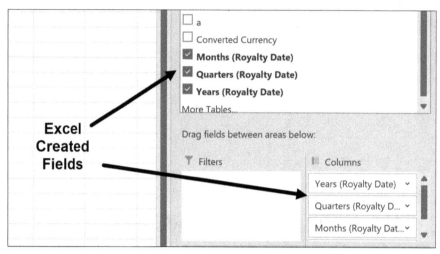

This is either going to be very useful to you or very annoying, depending on what you were trying to do.

I find it very useful, because usually I am not concerned that X event happened on a specific date; I am more interested that it happened in 2022 or in January of 2022. Which means I really like that Excel breaks my date data down for me automatically. Then I can just uncheck the fields it created that I don't want to use.

Once Excel creates those options for you, they'll still be listed as available fields that you can add to your table at any time.

Now, I mentioned in the quick tips section that when I wrote the first draft of this book I was able to get Excel to work with my date column no problem with that convert text to columns trick, but then it stopped working and nothing I did could get Excel to treat that column of values as a date for a pivot table.

I could see that the number for that cell was a date value. I could use it in math. But Excel treated each date as a unique value for my pivot table. (I eventually did a full repair on my version of Office, something I've never had to do before.)

Good news is that dealing with that led me to discover another option for displaying your dates by month, quarter, and year that I hadn't known before. (I do not in fact know everything. I am very lazy. I learn what I need and do it that way until I get stuck and need to learn a new way. Anyway.)

If Excel doesn't automatically create month, quarter, and year versions of your date values for you, but the entries are formatted as dates, right-click on one of the values in your table, and choose Group. That will bring up a Grouping dialogue box:

You can choose from there months, quarters, or years. (Days, hours, minutes, or seconds, too.) Click on the one you need, and then OK, and it will break your data down by those categories.

Now, be careful with this. Because I had dates as text and it let me do it but then showed the date values as 1905 dates. So you still need to go through all the steps to turn your date into a date entry in the data table first. But it seems to work even when Excel is being weird.

Insert Timeline

Insert Timeline creates a dialogue box that you can use to filter your pivot table in real-time based on a date field. It is also more visible than filtering. You can always see exactly which date criteria are being applied to a table.

To create a timeline, go to the Filter section of the PivotTable Analyze tab, and click on Insert Timeline. That will bring up the Insert Timelines dialogue box:

Timelines are only available for fields that Excel thinks are dates for pivot table purposes. So when you click on that option, the only fields that will show are those fields.

Click the checkbox for the one that you want, and then click OK.

Excel will then create a timeline dialogue box for that specific field that you can use to filter your pivot table:

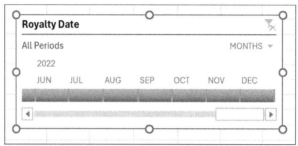

The range of values in the dialogue box will cover the entire date range of values for that field, even if some days, months, quarters, or years in the midst of the range have no data related with them. If you select days, months, quarters, or years that have no results, the pivot table will be blank.

There is a dropdown in the top right corner of the timeline that you can change to different time periods. If your dates cover it, you should be able to choose years, quarters, months, or days. After you do that, just click on the timeline to choose a specific value or range of values.

So I can do MONTHS, and then click on Jul for a specific year, and have only results for July of that year show in my pivot table.

If you want to select a range of months, days, years, etc., click on the starting value you want and hold down the Shift key while you click on the last value in you want.

Here, for example, I've selected January to March 2021:

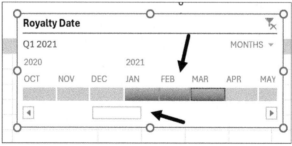

It is not possible to select non-contiguous dates. So you can't select June and October 2021, you have to select June *through* October.

There is a white outlined scroll bar below the date values that you can use to move through the entire range of available dates on the timeline.

To remove your timeline filter from your pivot table, just click on the funnel with an X in the top right corner of the dialogue box.

Right-click on the dialogue box and choose Remove Timeline to get rid of it. Your data may remain filtered if you were also using that field to build the table.

Insert Slicer

Insert Slicer lets you have a visible filter for all of your non-date fields. It can also be found in the Filter section of the PivotTable Analyze tab. Click on Insert Slicer, and then check the box for the field(s) you want to have a slicer for. Click OK when you're done.

Excel will insert slicers for each selected field. The slicers show all possible values for that field. Here, for example, are filters for net units sold and transaction type:

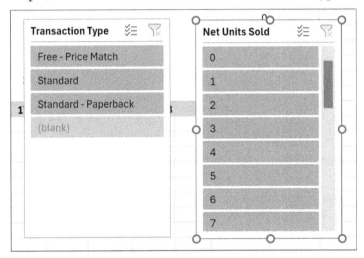

Click on a value to filter the pivot table by that value. Hold down the Ctrl key to select more than one value at once or the Shift key to select a range of values.

The multiselect option, at the top, next to the funnel, will let you choose more than one value without having to hold down the Ctrl key.

Turn off the filter by clicking on the funnel with an X in the top right corner.

Close the slicer by right-clicking and choosing the Remove option.

Grouping Row or Column Values

You can also manually group values in the rows or columns sections.

For example, in this data set I have three transaction categories: Free – Price Match, Standard, and Standard – Paperback. If I want to combine Standard and Standard-Paperback into one entry, I can do that.

To group values together, click on the first value you want in your group, and then hold down Ctrl and click on the other values you want to include.

Right-click when you have them all selected, and choose Group from the dropdown menu. (Or you can choose Group Selection from the Group section of the PivotTable Analyze tab.)

By default, Excel will give that new grouping the name Group1.

It will also assign all remaining values for that field to their own group with a group name that is identical to the value. For example, you can see here that I have a Group 1 that contains my two standard transaction types, as well as a group named (blank) that contains (blank) and one named Free – Price Match that contains Free – Price Match:

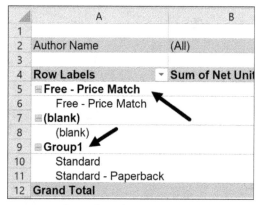

If you create more than one group for values in a field, Excel will just keep naming the groups with the next available number, so Group 2, Group 3, etc.

To change the name of a group, click on the name in the pivot table, go to the formula bar, and change the text in the formula bar to the name you want.

Here I'm clicked onto Cell A9 and have changed the name to Standard Transactions:

A9	fx	Standard Transactions	
	A		
1			
2	Author Name	(All)	
3			
4	**Row Labels**	**Sum of Net Units Sold Sum o**	
5	Free - Price Match		
6	Free - Price Match	91	
7	(blank)		
8	(blank)	1440	
9	**Standard Transactions**		
10	Standard	306	
11	Standard - Paperback	1043	

To add to an existing group, you need to select the fields that are already members of that group and then select the new values you want to include. So in the example above, I'd need to select Standard and Standard – Paperback, and then click on the field that was missing at that same level, and choose Group again..

To ungroup values, right-click on the group name, and choose Ungroup from the dropdown menu. Or click on the group name and then choose Ungroup from the Group section of the PivotTable Analyze tab.

See Underlying Data

If you ever need to see the specific entries from your original data table that led to a value in your pivot table, either double-click on that value, or right-click and choose Show Details.

Excel will create a new worksheet that has a data table showing all of the specific rows of data that led to that value:

	A	B	C	D	E	F	G	H	I
1	Royalty Date	Author Name	Marketplace	Transaction Type	Net Units Sold	Royalty	Currency	a	Converted Currency
2	2/1/2021	Author A	Amazon.co.uk	Standard	1	1.64	GBP		1.98
3	2/1/2021	Author A	Amazon.co.uk	Standard	1	1.64	GBP		1.98
4	2/1/2021	Author A	Amazon.co.uk	Standard	1	1.62	GBP		1.96
5	2/1/2021	Author A	Amazon.co.uk	Standard	1	1.67	GBP		2.02
6	2/1/2021	Author A	Amazon.co.uk	Standard	1	1.72	GBP		2.08
7	3/1/2021	Author A	Amazon.co.uk	Standard	0	0	GBP		0
8	6/1/2021	Author A	Amazon.co.uk	Standard	1	3.61	GBP		4.37
9	6/1/2021	Author A	Amazon.co.uk	Standard	1	2.13	GBP		2.58
10	7/1/2021	Author A	Amazon.co.uk	Standard	1	2.04	GBP		2.47

Be careful with this one, though, because when I was just playing with it, it did not adjust when I changed my entries in the original data table and tried to Refresh. There was no connection between the two anymore. This could be due to my security settings, or whatever was impacting Excel's ability to recognize my dates, but it's something to watch out for.

I think for my purposes, I would generate the detail, review it as needed, and then delete that worksheet immediately. If I need it again, it's just one click to create it.

Recommended Pivot Tables

In the Tools section of the PivotTable Analyze tab, there is an option for Recommended PivotTables. It takes your data and suggests some possible pivot tables to build with it. If you see something you like, just click on the one you want and then OK.

Personally, I don't use it because it doesn't save me time, but if you ever forget how to build a pivot table or aren't sure how to approach your data, it could be a good starting point.

Calculations

If you want to create a calculation within a pivot table, it is possible. To do so, go to the Calculations section of the PivotTable Analyze tab, and click on the dropdown arrow for Fields, Items & Sets, and choose Calculated Field.

You can then build a formula in the dialogue box that opens using the field names as your inputs

I rarely if ever use this and am going to assign it to an advanced use of Excel rather than walk you through it here. I just wanted you to know it exists if you ever think you need it. For me, personally, if I want to do more with my pivot table data, I copy and paste special-values and then go from there. The only reason I'd do calculations in a pivot table was if I expected to use that pivot table with data that was going to update periodically and that's just not something I've ever needed in 30 years of doing some pretty intensive data analysis in Excel.

Pivot Tables – Formatting

I do format my pivot tables in Excel, especially if I'm going to copy and paste that data for further use elsewhere. The two biggest changes I make are to remove subtotals and grand totals and to change my report layout to make the pivot table a data table.

Subtotals and Grand Totals

The default when you have multiple fields in rows or columns is for Excel to insert subtotals for you. Which is great if you're treating your pivot table as some sort of report. But I am often trying to get data I can then work with elsewhere, so I don't want those subtotals. It clutters things up, gets in the way, and I'd just want to delete them later,.

To remove any subtotals or grand totals used in your pivot table, go to the Layout section of the Design tab. You will see two dropdowns, Subtotals and Grand Totals. Here is the dropdown for Subtotals:

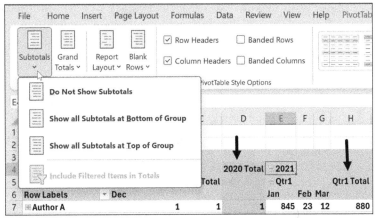

Click on the dropdown arrow for each one and select the option you want.

As you can see, for subtotals there are options for where your subtotals appear, "top" or "bottom". That means before the detail or after it. The default is top but sometimes I prefer it to be on the bottom.

Report Layout

To change how your data displays in your pivot table, go to the Layout section of the Design tab, and click on the Report Layout dropdown menu:

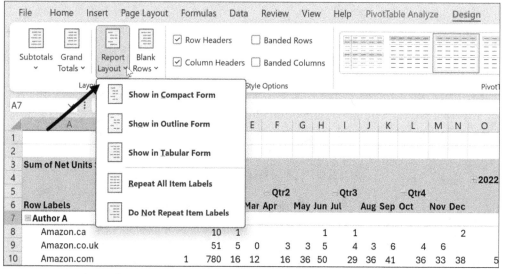

There are two sections there.

The top lets you decide if you want your pivot table rows to be Compact, which is the default, Outline format, or Tabular format. You can sort of see what the layout will look like in those little thumbnails, but I usually end up applying each one to find the one I want.

The second section lets you decide about repeating values for your columns.

By default, Excel does not repeat item labels. You can see below that 2021 shows once in Row 4, but not above each quarter and month that is part of 2021. Same with Qtr1 of 2021. Qtr1 shows once in Row 5 above Jan, but not above Feb and March. Fine for a report, but not for a data table that requires more analysis.

3	Sum of Net Units Sold	Column Labels															
4			2020	2021													2022
5			Qtr4	Qtr1			Qtr2			Qtr3			Qtr4				
6	Row Labels		Dec	Jan	Feb	Mar	Apr	May	Jun	Jul	Aug	Sep	Oct	Nov	Dec		
7	Author A		1	845	23	12	19	39	56	35	40	47	40	40	40		5
8	Author B			17			2	1									
9	Author C			90													
10	Author D		1	47		3	4	2	10	1	5	2	2	3			

To reformat a pivot table for data analysis I change the settings to Tabular form, Repeat Item Labels, no subtotals, and no grand totals. That gives me this:

	A	B	C	D	E
1					
2					
3	Sum of Net Units Sold		Years (Royalty Date)	Quarters (Royalty Date)	Months (Royalty Date)
4			2020	2021	2021
5			Qtr4	Qtr1	Qtr1
6	Author Name	Marketplace	Dec	Jan	Feb
7	Author A	Amazon.ca		10	1
8	Author A	Amazon.co.uk		51	5
9	Author A	Amazon.com	1	780	16
10	Author A	Amazon.com.au		2	
11	Author A	Amazon.com.mx			1
12	Author A	Amazon.es			
13	Author A	Amazon.fr			

Much better. I can now copy this worksheet and paste special – values into another worksheet, and have all of my rows and columns fully complete so I can do more analysis.

Other Formatting

Most of your pivot table formatting options will be in the Design tab. We already talked about the options on the left-hand side that cover subtotals, grand totals, and report layout. Now let's cover the rest:

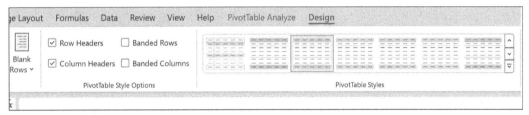

I want to start on the right-hand side with the PivotTable Styles section. If you look really close, you may be able to see that there is a box around the third option displayed there. That's because that is the current style that is by default being applied to my pivot table.

It has a color across the top row and the grand totals row at the bottom. When there are two fields used for rows, it also puts a light blue line between different values for the top-level field. (Not a row, a line.)

All but the first option in that first row are just different colored versions of that format. The first option uses a colored row to separate the different values when there are two levels in the row section.

If you look at the right-hand side there, you should see an up and a down arrow as well as a down arrow with a line behind it. Click on that arrow with the line behind it to see more formatting choices:

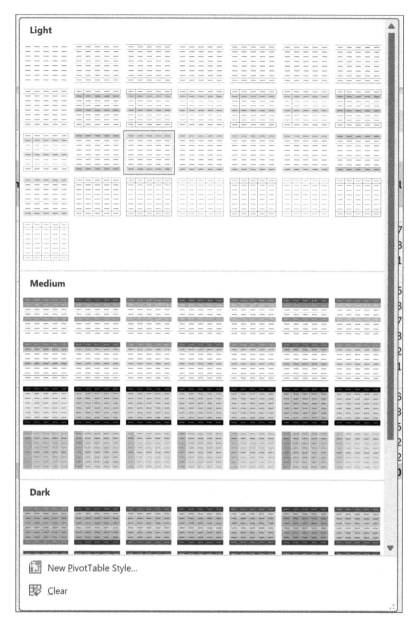

Hold your mouse over each one to see how it will look with your data (like I have on the next page).

If you like an option, click on it to apply.

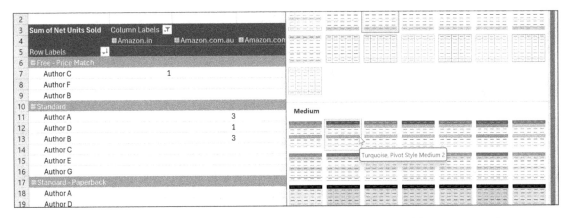

You should choose a style based upon the nature of the pivot table you created.

For example, some of the styles have a different format for the bottom row. Great if you have grand totals in your final row, but weird if you don't.

Same with the final column of the table. Some styles have a different format, which is great if you have a grand total column, but you shouldn't use it if you don't.

As you can see here, while I like this style and its color choices, the formatting isn't working with my data, because I do have a grand total column but this format doesn't treat that last column differently:

Sum of Net Units Sold	Column Labels							
	Amazon.in	Amazon.com.au	Amazon.com.mx	Amazon.com	Amazon.co.uk	Amazon.ca	Amazon Europe	Grand Total
Row Labels								
⊟ Free - Price Match								
Author C	1			78	1	3	4	87
Author F				3				3
Author B				1				1
⊟ Standard								
Author A		3	1	218	23	7	3	255
Author D		1		26	1			28
Author B		3		5	9			17
Author C				3				3
Author E				1			1	2
Author G					1			1
⊟ Standard - Paperback								
Author A				905	63	7	1	976
Author D				46	2			48
Author Z				5				5
Author B				1	1			2
Author E				2				2
Grand Total	1	7	1	1294	101	17	9	1430

I could try to find another style that works better. (You basically go down the column to find the varying styles and then across to find different color schemes.)

Or, I could start with this, and then customize it using the Font section of the Home tab.

In the table on the next page I bolded the last column, added fill color to the bottom row, changed my font color, and added a line to separate my left-most column and my right-most column. I also centered all of the numbers, and hid Rows 3 and 5:

	⊞ Amazon.in	⊞ Amazon.com.au	⊞ Amazon.com.mx	⊞ Amazon.com	⊞ Amazon.co.uk	⊞ Amazon.ca	⊞ Amazon Europe	Grand Total
⊟ Free - Price Match								
Author C	1			78	1	3	4	87
Author F				3				3
Author B				1				1
⊟ Standard								
Author A		3	1	218	23	7	3	255
Author D		1		26	1			28
Author B		3		5	9			17
Author C				3				3
Author E				1			1	2
Author G					1			1
⊟ Standard - Paperback								
Author A				911	67	8	1	987
Author D				50	2			52
Author E				2				2
Author B				1	1			2
Grand Total	1	7	1	1299	105	18	9	1440

Not bad. But you have to be careful when you depart from an existing pivot table style, because if you then change your data or refresh the table, you can lose some of that formatting. Not all, weirdly enough, but some.

So preferably save your formatting for last.

Custom Style

It is possible to create a customized pivot table style by going to the very bottom of the PivotTable Styles dropdown and clicking on New PivotTable Style.

That will bring up a dialogue box where you can fully customize the table appearance and save that customized look for use with the current table or any others in the workbook. If you're going to routinely update your data that feeds the pivot table and you don't like any of the default styles, you should either go with a default style or create a custom one.

If you choose to customize, in the dialogue box click on the name of each table element in the list, and then click on Format to bring up a Format Cells dialogue box, which will allow you to control any font attributes, borders, and fill colors. Make your choices, click OK, and then move on to the next element.

The Preview in the main dialogue box should show you what your table will look like with all of the elements formatted according to your choices.

If there is a style that already is partially what you want, right-click on it and choose Duplicate from the dropdown menu. That will start you with a style that already has all of that formatting applied, and you can then make additional changes from there.

When you're done, if you want all new pivot tables to automatically use the style you created, click on the Set As Default box at the bottom before you click OK.

* * *

Three more formatting options to discuss form the Design tab:

Blank Rows

The Blank Rows option in the Layout section of the Design tab lets you add blank rows between each grouped item in your rows. For a table like the one above it really doesn't do much, but if I take that same table and add a subtotal for each top-level category, then it does help a bit with visual separation:

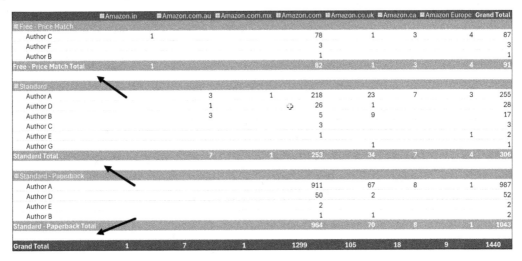

	Amazon.in	Amazon.com.au	Amazon.com.mx	Amazon.com	Amazon.co.uk	Amazon.ca	Amazon Europe	Grand Total
Free - Price Match								
Author C	1			78	1	3	4	87
Author F				3				3
Author B				1				1
Free - Price Match Total	1			82	1	3	4	91
Standard								
Author A		3	1	218	23	7	3	255
Author D		1		26	1			28
Author B		3		5	9			17
Author C				3				3
Author E				1			1	2
Author G					1			1
Standard Total		7	1	253	34	7	4	306
Standard - Paperback								
Author A				911	67	8	1	987
Author D				50	2			52
Author E				2				2
Author B				1	1			2
Standard - Paperback Total				964	70	8	1	1043
Grand Total	1	7	1	1299	105	18	9	1440

Banded Rows and Banded Columns

You can add banded rows or banded columns to any pivot table from the PivotTable Style Options section of the Design tab. Banded just means that every other column or row will be a different color. For example, here is banded columns:

4		Amazon.in	Amazon.com.au	Amazon.com.mx
6	Free - Price Match			
7	Author C	1		
8	Author F			
9	Author B			

See how every other column is a different color?

Here is banded rows:

4		Amazon.in	Amazon.com.au	Amazon.com.mx
6	Free - Price Match			
7	Author C	1		
8	Author F			
9	Author B			

The appearance of banded rows or columns is going to vary depending on the PivotTable Style you're using. For this style, for example, clicking both banded rows and columns just added a nice little line around each cell:

4		Amazon.in	Amazon.com.au	Amazon.com.mx	Amazon.com
6	Free - Price Match				
7	Author C	1			78
8	Author F				3
9	Author B				1

But for other styles it has a much bigger impact and I wouldn't recommend using both at the same time.

When choosing which one to use, if you think your data will primarily be read left to right, then banded rows can create good visual separation that makes that easier to do. If you think your data will primarily be read top to bottom, then banded columns will help.

Row and Column Header Formatting

There are also checkboxes in the PivotTable Style Options section of the Design tab for row headers or column headers. What unchecking those boxes does will depend on the style you chose. I recommend just clicking on them to see what you get.

* * *

We'll circle back to pivot tables later to cover pivot charts, but for now let's move on to conditional formatting, with a quick stop to learn how to create a two-variable analysis grid first.

Two-Variable Analysis Grid

Before we move on to our next tool in Excel, conditional formatting, I want to real quickly show you how to build what I call a two-variable analysis grid.

This is a table of values that represent the outcome of combining two different variables. For example, hours worked and pay. The higher your pay, the less you need to work to make the same amount, right? Or you can make up for earning less per hour by working more hours.

A two-variable analysis grid puts that information into a very practical lookup table which is simple to build, and which I'm going to use in the next chapter.

Okay. First thing you need to do is build the table with the values you want to use:

	A	B	C	D	E	F	G	H	I
1					Hours Worked				
2			20	25	30	35	40	45	50
3		$15							
4		$20							
5	Pay Rate	$25							
6		$30							
7		$35							
8		$40							
9		$45							
10		$50							

Building this involved a lot of the basic formatting we already covered in *Excel 2024 for Beginners*. I merged and centered the header sections across the cells, added fill color, changed the font color, centered the values I wanted to use, changed the text orientation along the left-hand side, and added borders:

Now we need to figure out the formula. In this case it's pretty basic, because we want to multiply hours times pay. In Cell C3 that would be:

$$=B3*C2$$

so I typed that in there.

Now, here's the fun part. We don't have to rewrite that formula for every cell in the table. Instead, we can change the formula so that it continues to reference Row 2 and Column B, but adjusts otherwise. Then we can just copy it.

You do that by putting a dollar sign in front of the part of each cell reference that you want to keep the same. Like so:

$$=\$B3*C\$2$$

I put a dollar sign in front of the B in B3 and in front of the 2 in C2. Now when I copy that formula to all of the other cells in the table, the formula in each cell will continue to reference Column B and Row 2 but will otherwise adjust. Like this:

	A	B	C	D	E	F	G	H	I
1					Hours Worked				
2		20	=C2+5	=D2+5	=E2+5	=F2+5	=G2+5	=H2+5
3	15	=$B3*C$2	=$B3*D$2	=$B3*E$2	=$B3*F$2	=$B3*G$2	=$B3*H$2	=$B3*I$2
4	=B3+5	=$B4*C$2	=$B4*D$2	=$B4*E$2	=$B4*F$2	=$B4*G$2	=$B4*H$2	=$B4*I$2
5	=B4+5	=$B5*C$2	=$B5*D$2	=$B5*E$2	=$B5*F$2	=$B5*G$2	=$B5*H$2	=$B5*I$2
6	=B5+5	=$B6*C$2	=$B6*D$2	=$B6*E$2	=$B6*F$2	=$B6*G$2	=$B6*H$2	=$B6*I$2
7	=B6+5	=$B7*C$2	=$B7*D$2	=$B7*E$2	=$B7*F$2	=$B7*G$2	=$B7*H$2	=$B7*I$2
8	=B7+5	=$B8*C$2	=$B8*D$2	=$B8*E$2	=$B8*F$2	=$B8*G$2	=$B8*H$2	=$B8*I$2
9	=B8+5	=$B9*C$2	=$B9*D$2	=$B9*E$2	=$B9*F$2	=$B9*G$2	=$B9*H$2	=$B9*I$2
10	=B9+5	=$B10*C$2	=$B10*D$2	=$B10*E$2	=$B10*F$2	=$B10*G$2	=$B10*H$2	=$B10*I$2

The formula in Cell I10 is

$$=\$B10*I\$2$$

Pretty cool, huh?

(You can see all the formulas in a worksheet by going to the Formulas tab and clicking on Show Formulas under Formula Auditing. That's why you can also see that I built the values used in the table with formulas. I told you, I'm lazy.)

Here are the actual results of the calculations:

C3			fx	=$B3*C$2				
	A	B	C	D	E	F	G	H	I
1					Hours Worked				
2			20	25	30	35	40	45	50
3		$15	$300	$375	$450	$525	$600	$675	$750
4		$20	$400	$500	$600	$700	$800	$900	$1,000
5		$25	$500	$625	$750	$875	$1,000	$1,125	$1,250
6		$30	$600	$750	$900	$1,050	$1,200	$1,350	$1,500
7		$35	$700	$875	$1,050	$1,225	$1,400	$1,575	$1,750
8		$40	$800	$1,000	$1,200	$1,400	$1,600	$1,800	$2,000
9		$45	$900	$1,125	$1,350	$1,575	$1,800	$2,025	$2,250
10		$50	$1,000	$1,250	$1,500	$1,750	$2,000	$2,250	$2,500

Do the math yourself, and you'll see that it worked for each of the cells.

Okay, now let's go use this table to demonstrate conditional formatting.

Conditional Formatting

Conditional formatting is a great way to visualize differences in your data. You can think of it as having Excel go through your results and highlight or otherwise call out results that meet various criteria. Just this week I used it to identify some duplicates in a list of values I had, but more often I use it to identify the "best" or "worst" in a range or to show how a range of values compare to one another.

Let's dive in and look at some examples because this one is very visual.

Looking at the analysis grid we built in the last chapter, let's say we know that you need to earn at least $1,200 a week. We can use conditional formatting to analyze the results in that table and color code them so that all values over $1199 are shaded in green.

Here that is:

	A	B	C	D	E	F	G	H	I
1					Hours Worked				
2			20	25	30	35	40	45	50
3		$15	$300	$375	$450	$525	$600	$675	$750
4		$20	$400	$500	$600	$700	$800	$900	$1,000
5	Pay Rate	$25	$500	$625	$750	$875	$1,000	$1,125	$1,250
6		$30	$600	$750	$900	$1,050	$1,200	$1,350	$1,500
7		$35	$700	$875	$1,050	$1,225	$1,400	$1,575	$1,750
8		$40	$800	$1,000	$1,200	$1,400	$1,600	$1,800	$2,000
9		$45	$900	$1,125	$1,350	$1,575	$1,800	$2,025	$2,250
10		$50	$1,000	$1,250	$1,500	$1,750	$2,000	$2,250	$2,500

This makes it much easier to see what combinations of hours and pay reach your goal. Basically, for this range of hours worked, you need a minimum of $25 an hour, and that only gets you to your goal if you work at least 50 hours. On the higher end, $50 an hour is great as long as you get at least 20 hours.

Very useful. So let's walk through all the many, many choices you have for conditional formatting of your data.

Apply

There are five categories of conditional formatting: Highlight Cells Rules, Top/Bottom Rules, Data Bars, Color Scales, and Icon Sets

To apply conditional formatting, select the range of cells you want to apply it to, click on the arrow next to Conditional Formatting in the Styles section of the Home tab, hold your mouse over the category you want to use, and then click on the subcategory you want from the secondary dropdown menu:

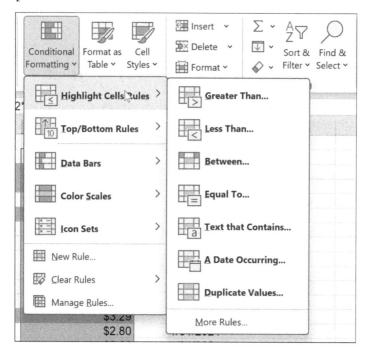

Most options will bring up a dialogue box where you can enter specific criteria and choose a format. Enter the criteria you want to use, choose the format you want, and then click OK. (We'll walk through this in much more detail in a moment.)

Usually I will apply one of the defaults and then go in and edit from there if I want something different in terms of criteria. For example, you may have wondered above why I did over $1199 instead of equal to or greater than $1200. It's because, as you can see in the secondary dropdown menu above, greater than is one of the listed choices, whereas greater than or equal to requires a little more effort to apply.

(In the main dropdown menu, the New Rule option will bring up the New Formatting Rule dialogue box which gives you more choices but also takes more effort.)

Okay, so let's walk through each of the five categories now.

Highlight Cells Rules

You can see the secondary menu for highlight cell rules on the prior page.

Greater Than, Less Than, Between, and Equal To

The first four options there are Greater Than, Less Than, Between, and Equal To. They work pretty much the same. Select the one you want and you'll see a dialogue box. This is the one for Between:

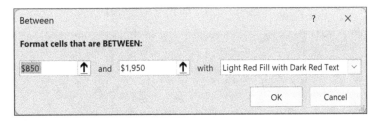

Excel guesses the values you might want to use, but you can just click into each box and type the value you want.

The dropdown on the right-hand side tells you how cells that meet that criteria will be formatted. The default is Light Red Fill with Dark Red Text. The other pre-formatted choices are Yellow Fill with Dark Yellow Text (which I have never used in my life), Green Fill with Dark Green Text, Light Red Fill, Red Text, and Red Border.

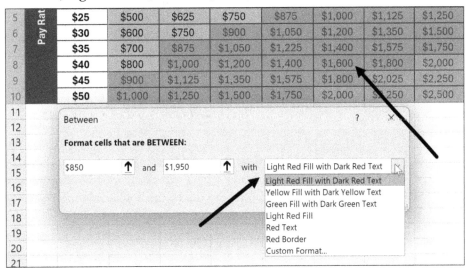

As you can see, whoever put the defaults together assumed you'd mostly want to flag "bad" things since red tends to mean bad in the U.S., especially when used with yellow and green. I personally want to flag things green often, so I almost always have to use that dropdown menu.

If you choose the last item in that dropdown, Custom Format, that will bring up a Format Cells dialogue box where you can apply pretty much any formatting you want to the cells that meet your criteria. If you want purple bolded text with a green striped background, go for it.

(Stripes are under the Pattern Style dropdown on the Fill tab. But just because you can do something does not mean it's actually a good idea to do it. Just sayin'.)

Text That Contains

The highlight cells rules secondary dropdown also has an option for text that contains something. Click on that to get the dialogue box and then type in the text you want. Like so:

1	Royalty Da	Author Nar	Marketplace	Transactiœt	Units So	Royalty	Currency
2	2021-01-31	Author A	Amazon.com	Standard	1	5.70	USD
3	2021-01-31	Author B	Amazon.com.au	Standard	1	5.03	AUD
4	2021-01-31	Author C	Amazon.com	Free - Price	65	0.00	USD
5	2021-01-31	Author D	Amazon.com	Standard	1	2.76	USD
6	2021-01-31	Author C	Amazon.fr	Free - Price	1	0.00	EUR
7	2021-01-31	Author C	Amazon.ca	Free - Price	3	0.00	CAD
8	2021-01-31	Author A	Amazon.com	Standard	1	5.83	USD
9	2021-01-31	Author C	Amazon.de	Free - Price	3	0.00	EUR
10	2021-01-31	Author A	Amazon.com	Standard	1	1.75	USD
11	2021-01-31	Author A	Amazon.com	Standard	1	2.74	USD
12	2021-01-31	Author A	Amazo				

Text That Contains   ?   ✕

Format cells that contain the text:

USD| ↑   with   Light Red Fill with Dark Red Text   ⌄

OK   Cancel

Note that Excel is applying the conditional formatting in the background even though I haven't yet clicked on OK. Pay attention to this to make sure you're getting the result you want.

I just tested this, and it is not case sensitive.

It will also work with a cell reference, so if the text you want is in a cell in your worksheet, you can click on that cell rather than type the text into the dialogue box.

And it works with wildcard characters. So if I have entries for USD and .com.usd, and I want that second one only, I can type ?usd into the field. Excel will only highlight cells where there is some text in front of usd.

I could also use usd? as my input to only return entries where there is something beyond usd in a cell.

A Date Occurring

Another option in the highlight cells rules secondary dropdown is for a date occurring, but I find this one of limited use because of the choices it gives you:

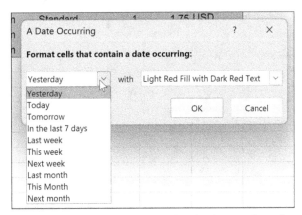

The choices there are yesterday, today, tomorrow, in the last 7 days, last week, this week, next week, last month, this month, and next month. Those are great choices for someone trying to use conditional formatting for something like receivables or payables. You are owed money and you want to see who is past due. Or you need to pay some bills and you want to see which ones are due in the next week so you can pay them.

But I often work with older data sets than that, and as far as I know there's no customizing this one beyond these choices.

Duplicate Values

The final option in that secondary dropdown is for Duplicate Values. I recently used this for a data analysis because I had multiple entries for some case numbers, and I wanted to quickly look at those duplicates to see if they were legitimate, or if someone had double-entered information. This worked well for that because my data was sorted by case number and so the duplicates were right next to each other.

Where it doesn't work as well is when the data is more spread out. Because if you have 10, 10, 20, 20, 30, and 30 at different points in your data, Excel will highlight all six cells the same color even though you technically have three distinct sets of duplicate values.

It also doesn't work as well where there are lots of duplicates.

But for something like subtotals where you want to make sure you didn't have any repeats, it can be pretty useful:

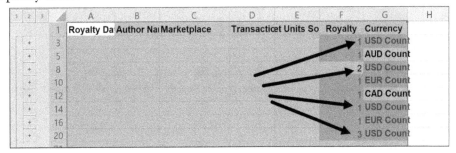

Top/Bottom Rules

Our next category of rules are the top/bottom rules:

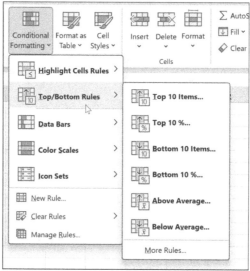

Note that each of the options there in the secondary dropdown uses 10. So top 10, bottom 10, top 10%, bottom 10%. The reality is that when the dialogue box comes up, you can choose whatever number you want to use. Here I changed the value to 3 instead, for example:

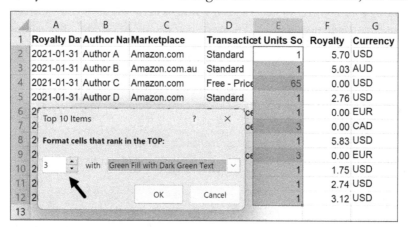

(I also changed the color.)

This dropdown also includes a choice for flagging above average and below average results. The average value it will work off is the average you can see in the bottom right corner of your worksheet when your cells are selected.

In this example that is 8, so most of my cells are highlighted as below average because I had a couple of big numbers in the mix:

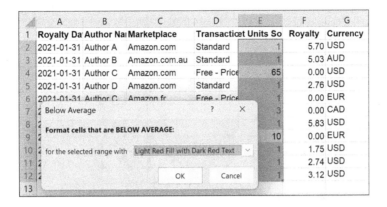

Data Bars

The next category of conditional formats is Data Bars. The secondary dropdown for this one just gives you a choice between solid bars and gradient bars in a variety of colors. By default, he longer the bar the higher the value compared to the other selected cells.

Initially, Excel will determine the range of values to use based on the values in your selected range. Click on More Rules at the bottom of the secondary dropdown menu to set those values yourself via the New Formatting Rule dialogue box:

This is also where you can tell Excel to just display the bars and not the associated numbers.

Here are three examples of the green gradient data bar option applied to ten values, but with different settings:

Default	Bars Only	Range of -20 to 20
1		-5
2		-12
3		3
4		4
5		5
6		6
7		7
8		8
9		9
10		10

The first two have values from 1 to 10. The first column is the default data bar setting where the bar gets larger as the number increases, until it fills the cell when the number is the largest in the range. The second is the exact same, except I chose to hide the actual numbers.

With the third one, I made the first two entries negative numbers, and then changed the criteria to say that the range for the data bars was -20 to 20. Since my largest positive value is 10, that cell's bar only covers a fourth of the cell width, half of the positive side. With my negative numbers, the data bar is red by default and, again, doesn't go to the end because the smallest number is -12 but I told Excel the range should go to -20.

Color Scales

Another way to visually see differences across your data is to use color scales. I like to use this one for my monthly revenue, ad cost, and profit numbers. It lets me quickly scan multiple years of monthly values for each, and see if things are going up or down based upon the darkness of each cell.

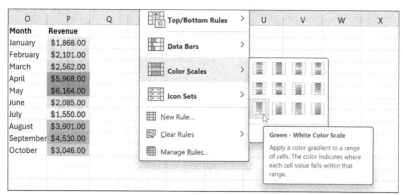

This is another one where you're basically just choosing your color scheme in the secondary dropdown men.

There are a variety of choices that involve green, red, and yellow as well as a couple that involve red, white, and blue instead. I prefer to use a custom color range, because to me red is bad and green is good, so applying a color scheme that uses red and green implies that you've "failed" for the red values and "succeeded" for the green values. But maybe none of them are good. Or maybe all of them are good. So I tend to use different shades of teal or orange or something like that. Like this:

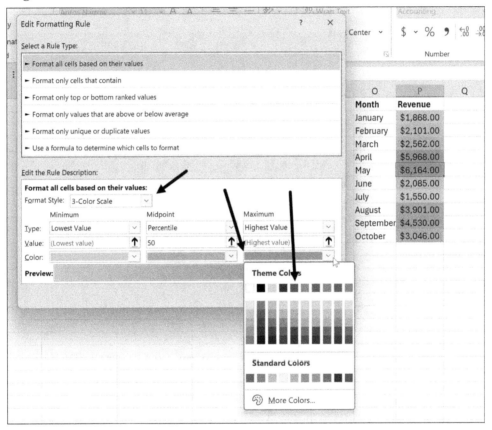

Here I edited the Format Style to use three colors. I then chose the first three colors in that fifth column of the theme colors dropdown menu to create my custom gradient. This blue color is neutral to me in terms of "bad" or "good", but at the same time the difference between the lighter fill color and darker fill color still tells me which months performed the best comparatively.

The default on this one is for Excel to use a percentile to bucket values around the minimum and maximum values in the range, but you can change that. It's possible to set specific numbers instead.

Icon Sets

The final way to visually represent your values is to use icon sets. Icon sets are basically images instead of colors. (Although many of the images also have colors as part of their composition.)

The secondary dropdown menu on this one allows you to choose the images you want to use.

Here I've chosen the "3 Traffic Lights" option that puts a green circle next to the highest values, a yellow one next to those in the middle, and a red one for the lowest values:

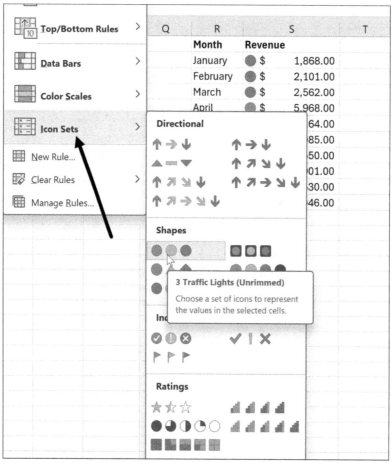

This is another one where if you're going to use it you probably want to customize the ranges used. The default is for Excel to take the values in the range, assign "good" to the top 33%, "okay" to the next 33%, and "bad" to the bottom 33%.

You can also set this one to just show the icons and not the values.

And you can also choose a different icon for each of the three buckets, but I wouldn't recommend it. They're grouped together for a reason.

Manage Conditional Formatting Rules

If you want to edit an existing rule, go to the Conditional Formatting dropdown menu, and choose Manage Rules. That will bring up the Conditional Formatting Rules Manager dialogue box:

At the very top, you can see the dropdown menu for which rules to display. The default is "Current Selection," but you can change that to your current worksheet, any other worksheet in your workbook, or any pivot table in your workbook.

Above, I chose This Worksheet. I also clicked and dragged from the bottom of the dialogue box to make it big enough to show all of the conditional formatting rules I have applied to this worksheet.

Below that dropdown is a row with four main options: New Rule, Edit Rule, Delete Rule, and Duplicate Rule. There is also an up arrow and a down arrow.

And below that is the list of all conditional formatting rules that apply for your selection.

The first column for each rule shows the type of rule (Icon Set, Graded Color Scale, Data Bar, etc).

The next column shows the formatting each rule is using.

The third column shows which cells each rule applies to.

The fourth column has a checkbox for "Stop if True". The checkbox is for situations where you have more than one conditional formatting rule applied to the same cell range. Excel will work through the rules from top to bottom but stop if that box is checked, and the rule was triggered by the contents in the cell.

Edit Rule

To edit a rule that you've already created, click on its row in the rules manager, and then click on Edit Rule at the top of that dialogue box.

That will bring up the Edit Formatting Rule dialogue box. Make the changes you want, click on OK, and you will be brought back to the Rules Manager dialogue box.

If that's all you wanted to do, click OK, the Rules Manager dialogue box will close, and your rule changes will be applied.

If you're not done, you can click Apply to apply that change immediately, or wait until you're done all of your changes and click OK to apply all of them at once.

Above, with the highlight cells rules, if I had wanted to format based on whether the values were greater than or equal to $1200 (instead of greater than $1199), I would have applied one of the default options, and then come here and edited that rule.

As you can see below, the dropdown in the Edit Formatting Rule dialogue box for highlight cell rules, contains greater than or equal to, less than or equal to, and not equal to:

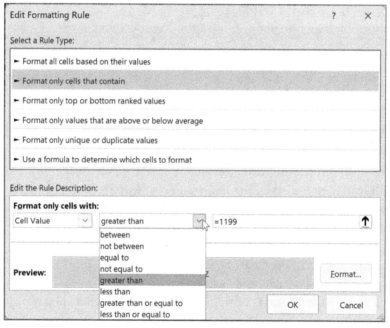

As you can see on the next page, the Edit Formatting Rule dialogue box for the "text that contains" rule will allow you to also format cells not containing, beginning with, or ending with your specified text:

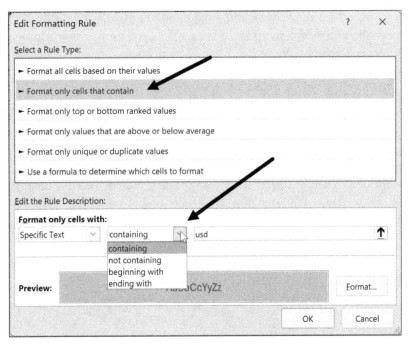

For the top/bottom rules, the Edit Formatting Rule dialogue box also lets you use standard deviations to flag your results:

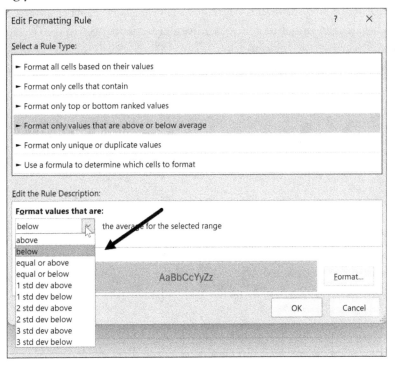

You can also reach the Edit Formatting Rule dialogue box by choosing More Rules at the bottom of any of the secondary dropdown menus, but if you use that option, you may have to change your category to find the correct list of options.

(Also note that you could build these rules from scratch by choosing New Rule from the main conditional formatting dropdown menu at the start, and then choosing the rule type you want, and going from there. I just find it easier to let Excel do most of the work first.)

Clear Rules

To remove conditional formatting, in the main conditional formatting dropdown menu you can hold your mouse over Clear Rules, and then choose to clear rules from the entire worksheet or the selected range of cells.

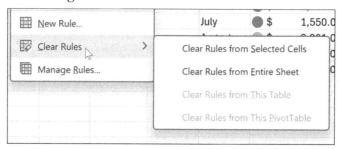

Your other option is to use the Rules Manager dialogue box. If you have a lot of cells that contain conditional formatting, but other conditional formatting you don't want to lose in that worksheet, that's probably the best option.

Delete Rule

To delete a rule, bring up the Conditional Formatting Rules Manager dialogue box by clicking on Manage Rules in the main conditional formatting dropdown menu. Click on the row for the rule you want to delete, and then click on Delete Rule at the top.

Duplicate Rule

To duplicate a rule, bring up the Conditional Formatting Rules Manager dialogue box, click on the row for the rule you want to duplicate, and then click on Duplicate Rule at the top.

Excel will put an exact duplicate of that rule at the top of your rules list. Use Edit Rule to make changes to it. (Or choose Cancel at the bottom to close the dialogue box without saving your changes.)

Multiple Rules On One Cell Range

It is possible to apply multiple conditional formatting rules to the same range of cells. For example, here I've applied red formatting to cells that are under $1,000 and kept the green formatting for cells over $1,199:

	A	B	C	D	E	F	G	H	I
1					Hours Worked				
2			20	25	30	35	40	45	50
3	Pay Rate	**$15**	$300	$375	$450	$525	$600	$675	$750
4		**$20**	$400	$500	$600	$700	$800	$900	$1,000
5		**$25**	$500	$625	$750	$875	$1,000	$1,125	$1,250
6		**$30**	$600	$750	$900	$1,050	$1,200	$1,350	$1,500
7		**$35**	$700	$875	$1,050	$1,225	$1,400	$1,575	$1,750
8		**$40**	$800	$1,000	$1,200	$1,400	$1,600	$1,800	$2,000
9		**$45**	$900	$1,125	$1,350	$1,575	$1,800	$2,025	$2,250
10		**$50**	$1,000	$1,250	$1,500	$1,750	$2,000	$2,250	$2,500

If the formatting you apply has no conflict, that's all you have to do. Just select that same range of cells twice and choose your formatting you want for each set of criteria.

But if you have rules that are applied to one cell range where there's a potential for conflict between the rules, then that's where you need to use the up and down arrows in the rules manager and/or the checkbox for Stop if True to make sure that when there's a conflict the correct rule takes precedence.

Conditional Formatting on Pivot Tables

It is possible to apply conditional formatting on a pivot table. To get started, it works the same way. Go to the pivot table, select the cells that you want to apply your formatting to, and apply your conditional formatting. (Be careful not to select subtotal and grand total fields, though.)

By default, Excel is going to set the range of cells covered by your pivot table conditional formatting to just the cells you selected. But for a pivot table, because they are dynamic, you very likely will want that to be set to a different option.

To do that, bring up the Conditional Formatting Rules Manager dialogue box by clicking on Manage Rules in the main conditional formatting dropdown menu.

Select the rule from the list, and choose Edit Rule.

That will give you a set of three options to choose from:

	Author E	Author F	Author G	(blank)	Grand Total
					$108.12
			$0.42		$451.74
	$14.71	$0.00			$6,179.57

Edit Formatting Rule

Apply Rule To: =$B$6:$I$16

◉ Selected cells

○ All cells showing "Sum of Converted Currency" values

○ All cells showing "Sum of Converted Currency" values for "Marketplace" and "Author Name"

Select a Rule Type:

► Format all cells based on their values

The first is the selected cells. The second is for all cells showing values for that field. The third is for the specific interaction between that field and any others you used to build the values in the table.

In this case that third option is for Sum of Converted Currency for Marketplace and Author Name. That's the one I want. That way if I add a new author or a new marketplace and refresh my pivot table, the conditional formatting will incorporate those changes.

* * *

Okay, so that was conditional formatting. It's a nice, easy way to flag your values in a data table to visually highlight what that data is telling you. But sometimes you don't want to have to show people the gory details of your data. In those cases, charts are a great way to visually summarize a lot of data. Let's cover those next.

Charts - Types

Okay, our next big topic is charts, which are yet another great way to visualize data. Sometimes taking a thousand rows of numbers and turning them into a pretty picture is truly the best way to understand what you're dealing with.

The way you build or format a chart is generally consistent across the various types of chart, but different charts are better used for different purposes, so I want to walk through chart types first, and then we'll get into how to actually insert charts and format them in the next chapter.

Let's start with a high-level summary for this chapter and then walk through examples.

Column charts, bar charts, and line charts are good choices for when you want to compare values using two different categories. For example, sales by store by month. The value is sales, the first category is store, the second category is month. I usually use these for time-series data where one of the categories is month, year, etc., but you don't have to. I could as easily use one of these chart types for sales by store for different formats (print, ebook, audio).

Pie, doughnut, and area charts are a good choice for when you're doing a "part of the whole" analysis. For example, total sales by store for a year. In that case, you want a visual that shows what part of the whole year's sales each store represented.

Scatter charts or histograms are a good way to visualize random data and look for patterns.

Okay, let's look at some actual charts now to help visualize what I just said. For most of this chapter the data table we'll be working with is this one that shows sales for four stores across six months and also includes totals for each store and for each month:

	A	B	C	D	E	F
1		Amazon	Kobo	Nook	Google	Total
2	January	$ 1,747	$ 353	$ 470	$ 65	$ 2,635
3	February	$ 1,616	$ 767	$ 445	$ 106	$ 2,934
4	March	$ 5,099	$ 420	$ 314	$ 1,132	$ 6,965
5	April	$ 4,596	$ 692	$ 140	$ 1,928	$ 7,356
6	May	$ 2,165	$ 809	$ 407	$ 1,090	$ 4,471
7	June	$ 2,502	$ 261	$ 244	$ 1,113	$ 4,120
8	Total	$ 17,725	$ 3,302	$ 2,020	$ 5,434	$ 28,481

(It's fake data so don't read anything into it or get hung up on if there's a weird number.)

First up:

Column and Bar Charts

Column and bar charts are essentially the exact same thing, it's just a question of whether the bars are vertical (column) or horizontal (bar). Excel includes both 2-D and 3-D versions of these charts.

In general, 3-D feels a bit gimmicky to me—like something that would be used in a bad consulting presentation. You do you, but if you're going to use 3-D, do it for a reason. (I do have an example of one possible use below and I have been known to be wrong before so there may be other uses out there.)

There are three main types of column and bar charts: clustered, stacked, and 100% stacked.

Clustered Charts

Here we have both a clustered column and a clustered bar chart that show the amount earned in each store for each month:

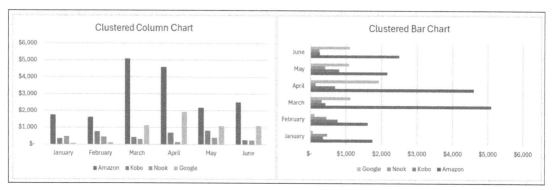

You can see that Excel created a separate column or bar for each store for each time period. The color of the column or bar stays the same for each store for each month, but the "height" of the column or bar varies month-to-month based on the sales for that particular store in that particular month.

Amazon, for example, is the darkest color. You can easily see that within each month Amazon had the highest sales compared to the other stores, but that it went up and down across the time period. You can also see that Google (the lightest colored column/bar) had a good month in April compared to its sales in other months.

Clustered columns are great for situations like this where you want to see the relative performance of a limited number of one category across a limited number of a second category. However, they can quickly get out of hand. Above, I have four stores and six months. That's easy enough to read. But imagine how busy this would get if I had ten stores across twenty-four months. It'd be a nightmare.

Also, note that it's pretty hard to see the *overall* change in sales month to month. You can see the obvious ones, like the increase from February to March, but what about March to April. Did total sales go up or down? It's not easy to see in this chart type. If that was something you needed to visualize, this chart would not be the best choice.

Stacked Charts

The next column and bar chart choice you have is a stacked chart:

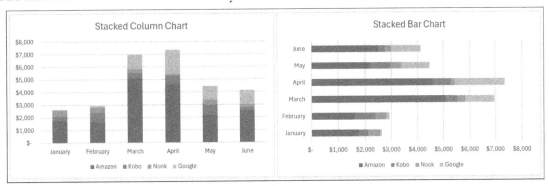

Stacked charts take the columns or bars used in clustered charts, and stack them on top of each other for each secondary category.

You can see here that instead of four separate columns or bars each month, there is one, and that each colored section in that one column or bar for the month represents the sales for a specific store for that month.

It's still possible to see relative performance between stores within a given month. But it can be harder to see how a specific store, like Google, did over time. Amazon is on the bottom so you can still see those changes month-to-month, but try matching up the sections for Kobo and comparing them to one another. Much harder to do.

The advantage to this chart type, though, is that you can easily see total performance across the time period much easier. Here we can immediately see that more was earned in April compared to March.

100% Stacked Charts

The next type of column or bar chart is the 100% stacked chart:

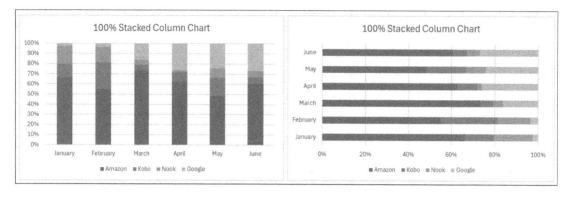

The column or bar "height" on this one is always going to be the same, because it always has to add up to 100%. In this case, the portion of the bar or column assigned to each store represents the *percent of the whole* for that store for that month. I mentioned before with pivot tables, that sometimes I'm not as concerned with total dollar value as I am with share of what was earned. Is one of my stores slipping so that even though my revenue is going up overall, that one store is in decline?

This chart type lets you see that better. Like the decline there March to April to May for Amazon. Why did Amazon's share of overall sales decline during those three months? Is this a good thing (I started selling better elsewhere) or a bad thing (my biggest source of revenue is in decline)?

I rarely use this chart type, though, because it can really hide key information. The problem with this chart type is that in one period you could have values of 1, 2, and 5, and in the next have 1000, 2000, and 5000, and they'd look exactly the same in the chart. If you're trying to pay your rent based on the amount you earn, the difference between making $8 in a month and $8,000 in a month is very important.

Same with disease analysis. Sure, it matters that Variant X is coming to dominate, but if Month 1 has 10,000 cases and Month 2 has 100, I think the 100 versus 10,000 is far more important than that the 100 comes 50% from Variant X instead of Variant Y.

3-D Column Chart

There is one type of column chart that is not mirrored as a bar chart, the 3-D Column Chart.

This one actually does provide information beyond what the standard 2-D charts provide, so I want to show it to you real quick.

The 3-D Column Chart is kind of like if you very carefully deconstructed the stacked column chart and put each piece that had been stacked one-by-one in a row behind the first piece. This lets you compare values for each store over time (left to right) as well as among stores for each month (front to back, back to front).

Here are two examples using the same data as above:

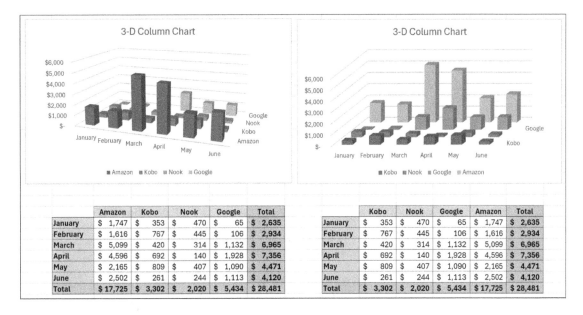

	Amazon	Kobo	Nook	Google	Total
January	$ 1,747	$ 353	$ 470	$ 65	$ 2,635
February	$ 1,616	$ 767	$ 445	$ 106	$ 2,934
March	$ 5,099	$ 420	$ 314	$ 1,132	$ 6,965
April	$ 4,596	$ 692	$ 140	$ 1,928	$ 7,356
May	$ 2,165	$ 809	$ 407	$ 1,090	$ 4,471
June	$ 2,502	$ 261	$ 244	$ 1,113	$ 4,120
Total	$ 17,725	$ 3,302	$ 2,020	$ 5,434	$ 28,481

	Kobo	Nook	Google	Amazon	Total
January	$ 353	$ 470	$ 65	$ 1,747	$ 2,635
February	$ 767	$ 445	$ 106	$ 1,616	$ 2,934
March	$ 420	$ 314	$ 1,132	$ 5,099	$ 6,965
April	$ 692	$ 140	$ 1,928	$ 4,596	$ 7,356
May	$ 809	$ 407	$ 1,090	$ 2,165	$ 4,471
June	$ 261	$ 244	$ 1,113	$ 2,502	$ 4,120
Total	$ 3,302	$ 2,020	$ 5,434	$ 17,725	$ 28,481

The reason I wanted to call this one out here is also because the order of your columns impacts the appearance.

In the left-hand 3-D chart, the tallest column is in front. This isn't because that is Excel's default. It's because Amazon was the first store listed in my data table, which I've added below the chart so you can see it.

In the right-hand 3-D chart, I moved Amazon's values to the last column. That put the largest values for each month in the back row and, I personally think, made the chart easier to read. Note, though, that it also changed the color assigned to Amazon and the other stores. That's because colors are just assigned down the line from first to last and Amazon is now last. (You can customize colors. We'll discuss that in the next chapter.)

Pie and Doughnut Charts

A doughnut chart is just a pie chart with the middle missing. I'd say pie charts are more of a traditional look while doughnut charts are more of a modern look, but it's the exact same information.

On the next page are examples using our data from above, that show share of total sales by store for the entire time period.

In both charts you can easily see that Amazon has the biggest share, and that Google is second. But note that these are part-of-the-whole-type charts, so you don't see actual values. You don't know if this is a chart of $8 in sales or $8,000 in sales.

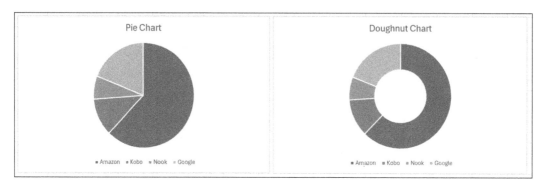

There are three other types of pie chart in Excel. One is a 3-D version, which I consider gimmicky. The others are a pie of pie chart and a bar of pie chart. I'll cover them so you understand them, but use them with caution.

Breakout Pie Charts

Pie of pie charts and bar of pie charts do the exact same thing, they break out a part of your data from your main pie chart into a separate chart. Here we have share of total sales by month in a standard pie chart, a pie of pie chart, and a bar of pie chart:

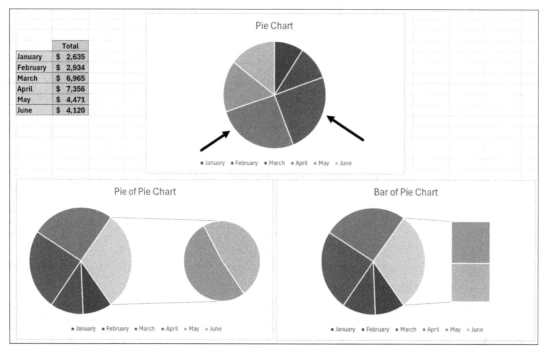

If you look at the standard pie chart, it's pretty easy to see that the two biggest months are March and April, the two bottom slices in the pie.

(In Excel you can hold your mouse over a chart element, like a pie slice, to see its label and value if you're not sure which color in the legend (guide) matches to that particular element. There are also formatting options to have Excel display labels and values on the chart itself that we'll cover in the formatting chapter.)

Okay. Now look at the pie of pie and bar of pie charts below that pie chart and try to figure out what you're seeing. It's the same information as in the basic pie chart.

If you just focused on the main pie chart in either one of those, you'd think that March and April, now on the left-hand side of the chart, are pretty much equal to that slice on the right-hand side, maybe even a little smaller. It would no longer be obvious that March and April were the best months because that third pie slice is just as big.

What is actually happening here is that the third pie slice there on the right side is a combination of two different months, May and June. And then that second chart on the right side, whether it be a pie chart or a bar chart, is just those two months charted against one another. (In other charts this could be many fields, but in this case Excel just chose those two.)

I do not find it intuitive to interpret these charts correctly. My natural inclination is to compare the size of the different slices to one another, which makes me think that May and June are the same size as March and April even though they're not.

The bar of pie chart is a little easier to understand, in my opinion, because it breaks that slice of the main pie chart into a bar chart, but I still think it's confusing because that secondary chart gives too much visual space to smaller values than it should.

I'm sure there are uses for these, just ask yourself before you use either one whether it helps explain your data or whether it causes confusion. If you're in a field where they get used often, most people will probably understand what you're doing, but if your chart has the chance to reach a wider audience, maybe find some other way to call out those smaller results, like a data table.

Also, these are good chart types to include labels with to help users understand what they're seeing. I have an example in the next chapter under Display Pie Chart Percent to show how I'd handle a pie of pie chart.

Line Charts

Line charts are great for seeing trends, but there are only two line charts I would recommend you use in Excel, Line and Line with Markers. The other line chart types Excel offers are stacked line charts like we looked at with column and bar charts, but they aren't intuitive. I'd avoid them and use area charts or bar or column charts instead. They're way too easy to misread.

Here is a Line chart showing total sales for each month:

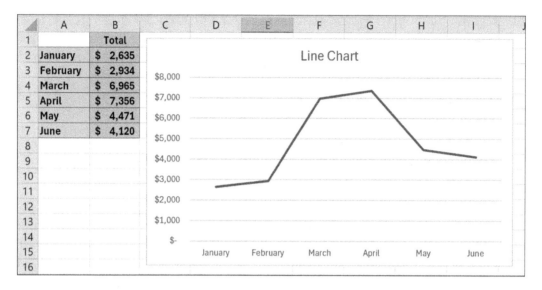

You can easily see how total sales were up in March and April, and how they stayed up a bit in May and June.

Here is a Line with Markers chart of sales for each store for each month:

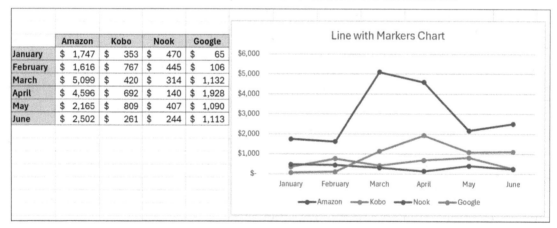

To include lines for each store, all I had to do was include the columns of data for the individual stores, Excel did the rest. The first column is the x-axis, the rest are charted against that.

Area Charts

We have all seen a lot of area charts over the last few years. Or maybe it's just me. A lot of the "share of variant" charts use an area chart to show which variants are gaining traction or fading away. Where the stacked line charts fail miserably, an area chart works. It basically creates a colored layer for each category where the width of the layer for a given period is determined by the value or percent of total for that period.

Here is a Stacked Area Chart and a 100% Stacked Area Chart for sales by store by month:

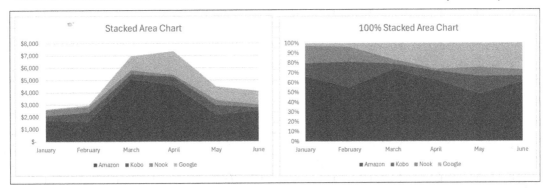

By filling in the space below each line, it becomes clear that the different pieces are stacked on top of one another to make a whole.

I think this chart type better shows the change for a specific store from period to period than a stacked column or bar chart, because even when a specific store is a small part of the whole, you can still see whether that layer gets bigger or smaller over time.

Of course, be careful once again with the 100% stacked chart since it doesn't show changes in overall total value. $8 and $8,000 can look the exact same.

Also, I'm thinking on this one that it's only good for time series data. I don't think I'd use it for sales by store by format, for example, because those don't really represent a continuum like time does. I looked online and found a few that broke that (like one that had car colors instead of months), but I think they were less successful than if they'd used a column or bar chart for that data instead.

Okay, next.

Scatter Plots

A scatter plot puts a dot on the chart for the intersection of two values. You can choose to just plot those dots (Scatter) or to plot those dots and connect them with a smooth line or a straight line (Scatter with Smooth Lines, Scatter with Straight Lines). If you connect dots with a line, you can also choose to include a marker for each data point (Scatter with Smooth Lines and Markers, Scatter with Straight Lines and Markers).

A scatter plot can be a good way to see clusters in data points or relationships between different data points. For this one we need new data points because a scatter chart is more likely to be used for random measurements of two variables than for the sales data we've been using.

On the next page is a basic scatter plot of nine data points:

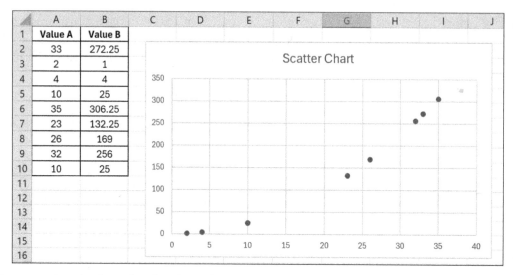

If I were to just look at the data in Columns A and B, I wouldn't be able to see that there's a relationship there. Maybe I could see that larger values of A also mean larger relative values of B, but that's about it. However, when I plot those values in a scatter chart, like I did above, suddenly we can see that there's a pattern there. Given the curve of that line, we also know it's likely exponential.

To confirm that, I really want to draw a line between those points. Problem is, if I do it with my data as it is now, it looks horrible:

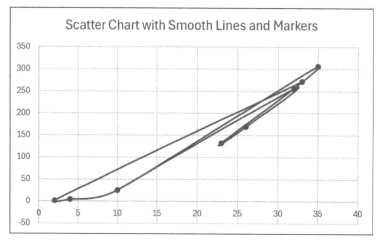

That's because Excel draws the connecting points between each line in order from first to last. It's basically assuming that there is a time component to the data you gave it, and that the order in which the data points were collected also matters.

If the order of the observations is not important, then sort your data before you create a scatter plot.

Here I sorted by the values in the first column and plotted again with a smooth line and it works:

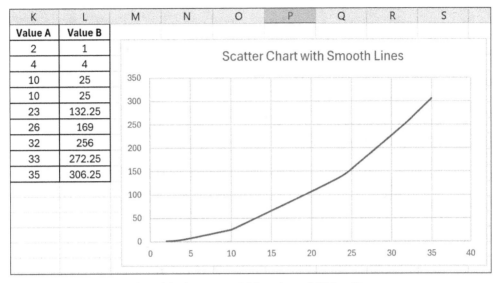

Value A	Value B
2	1
4	4
10	25
10	25
23	132.25
26	169
32	256
33	272.25
35	306.25

I can now clearly see a relationship between Value A and Value B.

With enough data points, the difference between smooth and straight lines becomes less important, but when you have fewer data points a straight line can more clearly show the lack of observations between two points.

It is also possible to have a scatter plot with more than two values plotted against the same base value. The first column of your data will be used to set the x-axis values, the remaining columns of data will then be plotted against the values in that first column.

Like this:

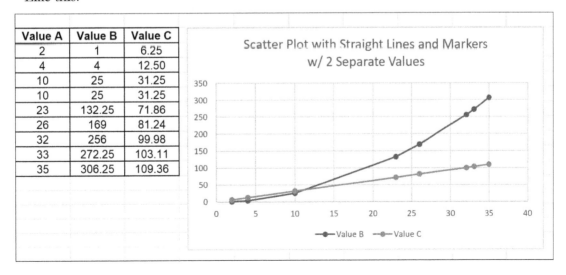

Value A	Value B	Value C
2	1	6.25
4	4	12.50
10	25	31.25
10	25	31.25
23	132.25	71.86
26	169	81.24
32	256	99.98
33	272.25	103.11
35	306.25	109.36

(You can do this without a line connecting the various points, but that might be a little hard to read because you'll just have a bunch of different colored dots on your plot.)

Bubble Plots

A bubble plot is like a scatter plot except you can have an additional value that is represented by the size of the bubble that plots each point.

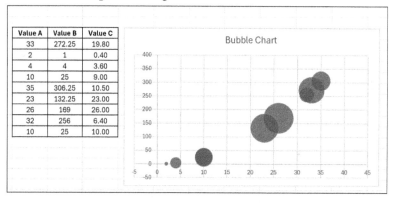

Histogram

Histograms take a set of values and place them into equally-sized buckets that cover the range of your data from smallest to largest. They're useful for seeing if there's a pattern to the distribution in your data. The more observations you have, the more clear any distribution will become.

Below we have two histograms, one with only 29 observations, the other with 100.

Both are using a data set that generates random whole numbers between the values of 5 and 60.

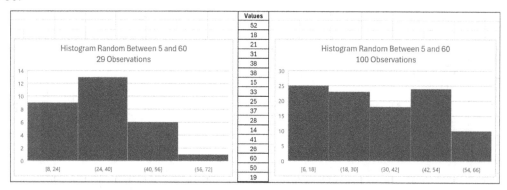

You can see that as the number of observations goes up, the buckets that Excel assigns get closer to the true range of the values. Also, the buckets start to even out in terms of the count of how many values fall into each bucket. With enough observations, we'd be able to see that the values are randomly distributed across that range.

With normally distributed data, the more observations you had the more the histogram would start to look like a standard bell curve.

It is possible to customize the range and number of buckets Excel uses for a histogram. We'll cover that in the next chapter.

Other Chart Types

Excel contains other types of charts such as a Treemap, a Sunburst, waterfall, surface, stock, radar, and box and whisker charts. You can also create maps that are filled in according to various values. I'm not going to delve into those here because I think most of the readers of this book won't need them. Just know that they exist if you do. (And remember that Excel actually has excellent help available on the Microsoft website as well as through the Help tab if you have the right settings enabled.)

Combo Charts

This is also just a quick mention. Excel lets you create combo charts so that you can combine two types of charts in one.

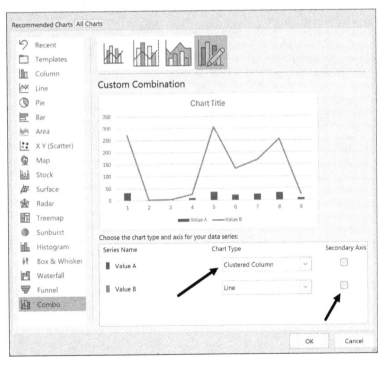

I was playing with this recently because I had downloaded a timeline template from the Office website and needed to understand how it worked.

What I figured out is that it was basically a line chart with values of zero paired with column charts that drew a bar for each point on the timeline. (Which meant that to get things lined up properly on the timeline I had to have my data points sorted by date, which was not obvious up front.)

It was a really interesting use of Excel. (That, me being me, I then expanded into using six different column charts so that I could color code different entries on the timeline.)

That's an advanced topic, though. Just know it exists if you want to try to go there at some point. And, if you do, use the secondary axis if your values are very different. (Like number of months and dollar value.)

Okay. Now that we've covered the different chart types, let's actually walk through how to create a chart and format it.

Charts – Insert and Format

Before you can create a chart, you need to format your data properly.

For column, bar, pie, and doughnut charts, you want to have labels across the first row and down the first column, and then your values in the cells in the table where those labels would intersect. Also, no subtotals or grand totals. If you do have grand totals, leave them out when you select your data.

As an example, this was the data table I worked with in the last chapter:

	A	B	C	D	E	F
1		Amazon	Kobo	Nook	Google	Total
2	January	$ 1,747	$ 353	$ 470	$ 65	$ 2,635
3	February	$ 1,616	$ 767	$ 445	$ 106	$ 2,934
4	March	$ 5,099	$ 420	$ 314	$ 1,132	$ 6,965
5	April	$ 4,596	$ 692	$ 140	$ 1,928	$ 7,356
6	May	$ 2,165	$ 809	$ 407	$ 1,090	$ 4,471
7	June	$ 2,502	$ 261	$ 244	$ 1,113	$ 4,120
8	Total	$ 17,725	$ 3,302	$ 2,020	$ 5,434	$ 28,481

For the bar and column charts, I selected Cells A1 to E7. For the pie and doughnut charts, I selected either Cells A2 to A7 and F2 to F7 (using the Ctrl key) or Cells B1 to E1 and Cells B8 to E8, depending on if I was looking at total sales by month or by store.

For the line graphs, scatter plots, bubble plots, and histogram, it was different. Those can work with one column of data. Put the label for the values in the first cell. If you want more than one line graph in a chart, or more than one set of data for a scatter plot, put the data in consecutive columns. The screenshots in the last chapter included examples.

Insert

Okay. Assuming you have a data table to work with, the first step for inserting a table is to select the cells that contain your data.

Next, go to the Charts section of the Insert tab, and find the dropdown menu for the chart type you want:

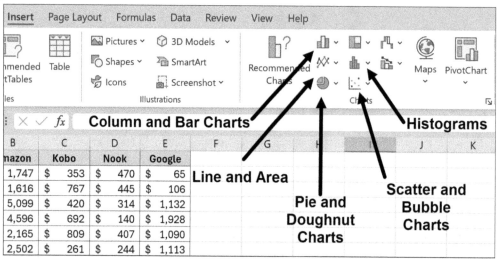

You can hold your mouse over each image on the menu tab as well as in the dropdown for each chart type, to see what kind of chart it is. This will also include a description of when it should be used. Here, for example, is the dropdown for column and bar charts where I am holding my cursor over the 2-D stacked column chart:

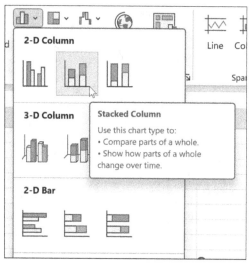

It says that the Stacked Column chart type is best to compare parts of a whole or to show how parts of a whole change over time.

If you have data selected when you hold your mouse over a chart type in the dropdown menu, the chart will appear in the background, allowing you to see what your data will look like. Click to actually insert it.

Another option, if you're not sure what type of chart to use, is to click on the Recommended Charts option in the Charts section of the Insert tab.

That will open the Insert Chart dialogue box to the Recommended Charts tab:

Click on the chart thumbnails on the left-hand side to see a larger sample of what your data would like like in that type of chart.

You should also see a description below the sample of what that chart type is meant to do.

Click OK to select the currently-displayed sample chart or Cancel to close without inserting a chart.

In that dialogue box, you can also click over to the All Charts tab at the top. That will show a listing of all the available chart types.

Click on a high-level chart type on the left, and then click on the icon for a specific chart type along the top, to see samples of what your data will look like using that specific chart type.

Here I've selected Bar on the left-hand side and Clustered Bar at the top:

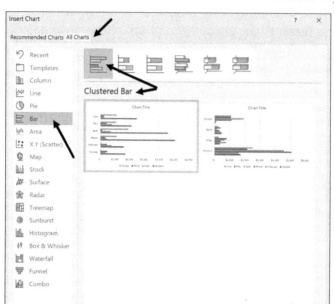

If you look at the sample charts in the All Charts section of the dialogue box, when there are two sample charts, like above, the left-hand image is usually how the chart will look with your data table formatted as is. The right-hand image is how the chart will look if you switch your row and column data.

In the image above, for example, the left-hand chart is sales by store by month and the right-hand chart is sales by month by store. (As we'll discuss soon, you can always switch row and column data after you insert a chart, too.)

Chart Menu Tabs

When you insert a chart into Excel and are clicked onto that chart, there will be two additional menu tabs available, Chart Design and Format.

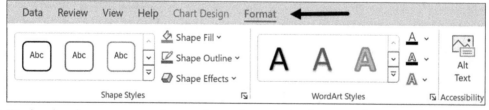

Chart Design is where you can choose the various chart elements for your chart, change your chart colors (like I've been doing throughout to make this print better in black and white), choose various suggested chart styles or layouts, switch your column and row data, change what data is being used in your chart, and change your chart type.

The Format tab is where you can manually change the formatting of your chart, such as the size or colors of different elements.

Chart Task Pane

It won't automatically be visible when you insert a chart, but there is also a chart task pane that will allow you to apply various formatting to the elements in your chart. We'll cover some of what you can do there, and how to open it, towards the end of this chapter.

＊ ＊ ＊

Okay. Let's start talking about how to edit an existing chart. First up, all the ways you can fix an error if you didn't quite get it right when you inserted your chart.

Switch Row/Column

Here is a chart I just inserted in Excel:

It shows sales by store for each month. But what if I had actually wanted sales by month for each store?

The easiest way to make that change is to go to the Data section of the Chart Design tab, and click on Switch Row/Column. Immediately, I get this:

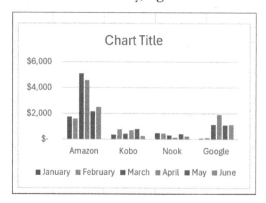

See how the axis is now the store names and the columns are now the months?

Change Data

What if you realize that you included fields in your chart that you didn't want to (like totals or subtotals), or you add more data after the fact and want to incorporate it?

For example, here I've added one more "store", Other.

	A	B	C	D	E	F
1		Amazon	Kobo	Nook	Google	Other
2	January	$ 1,747	$ 353	$ 470	$ 65	$ 50
3	February	$ 1,616	$ 767	$ 445	$ 106	$ 34
4	March	$ 5,099	$ 420	$ 314	$ 1,132	$ 123
5	April	$ 4,596	$ 692	$ 140	$ 1,928	$ 65
6	May	$ 2,165	$ 809	$ 407	$ 1,090	$ 228
7	June	$ 2,502	$ 261	$ 244	$ 1,113	$ 185
8						
9						
10		Chart Title				
11						
12	$6,000					
13	$4,000					

When you click on a chart, Excel will select the cells in your data table that are being used to create that chart.

Above, for example, Cells B1 through E1 are providing one of the categories, A2 through

A7 are providing the other, and B2 through E7 are providing the values. But note that none of the cells in Column F are currently selected.

One way to change the cells being used, is to left-click and drag from the bottom of the cell range that's already selected. In this case that would be the bottom right corner of Cell E7. (You may be able to see the angled, double-ended arrow there, but maybe not because it's a little small.)

When you left-click and drag to expand the selected cells, Excel should expand to capture both the header row and the cells with the values in them, but if it doesn't, then just do the same for the cell(s) with the header row value(s).

Another way to change your data, is to go to the Select Data option in the Data section of the Chart Design tab. Click on that to bring up the Select Data Source dialogue box:

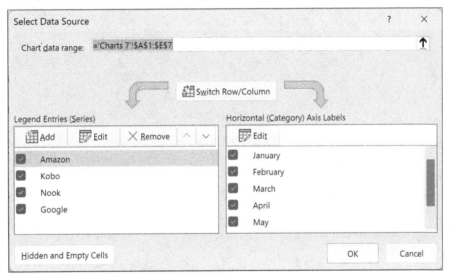

You can do a lot here, including switch your rows and columns, but if you're here to change your data, click into the Chart Data Range field at the top.

The Chart Data Range field does not work well if you click into it and try to use arrows. So one option is to click right next to the E, delete it, and replace it with an F.

The other is to select all of the text there now, delete it, and then go and select the correct cell range from your worksheet.

* * *

This dialogue box is also a great way to remove certain values from a chart after the fact.

For example, sometimes Amazon is so far out of range of the other stores for me, that having it in a chart obscures the detail for my other stores. When that happens, I open this dialogue box, and uncheck Amazon in the Legend Entries section on the left-hand side.

That removes the Amazon values from the chart.

* * *

This is also a place to go to fix the Legend Entries field names.

I generally recommend that you edit them in the data table itself, but sometimes that's not possible. If you need to edit them here, click on the value you want to change in the lower section of the Select Data Source dialogue box, and then click on the Edit option for that section.

This will bring up the Edit Series dialogue box:

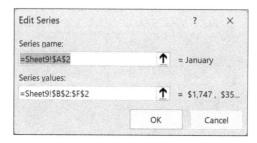

By default, the name fields will be cell references. You can see a sample value to the right.

For Legend Entries, click into the white box for Series Name, and type the label you want to use instead, and then click OK.

If you need to edit the Horizontal Axis Labels, that is a little different because it is a cell range, not a single cell. Instead of typing in one value, use curly brackets around your text, with commas to separate each entry.

{Entry 1, Entry 2, Entry 3}

For both, you can also replace the original cell reference or cell range reference with a different cell reference.

Use Cancel to close either of those dialogue boxes without making changes.

Change Chart Type

You can easily change an existing chart to a different chart type by clicking on the chart, and then using the Change Chart Type option in the Type section of the Chart Design tab.

Clicking on that will bring up a dialogue box that looks just like the Insert Chart dialogue box. From there, just find the chart type you want, click on it, and click OK.

* * *

Now that you have the chart set up the way you want, it's time to learn how to pretty it up.

Change Chart Title

If you've been trying things yourself as you read this book, you may have noticed that when a chart is inserted into Excel it has a default title of Chart Title. Not something you'll want to keep most of the time.

To change that title, click on it. You should see a box appear around the text. Select the text in that box by either left-clicking and dragging or using Ctrl + A, and then type the title you want.

You can format text in that box the same way as any other text in Excel using the Font section of the Home tab. That generally does everything I need for a chart title.

But if you want to get fancier, you can also use the WordArt Styles section of the Format tab to apply outlines to your text as well as special effects like shadow, reflection, and glow.

Another option for that is to right-click on your title box, and choose Format Chart Title from the dropdown menu. This will open a task pane on the right-hand side for Format Chart Title. Click around in the Title Options and Text Options to explore the choices available there.

Change Chart Colors (Easy Way)

To change your chart colors, an easy option is to click on the chart, and then go to the Chart Design tab. In the Chart Styles section, there is a dropdown menu for Change Colors.

Click on that to see almost 20 different pre-formatted color palettes:

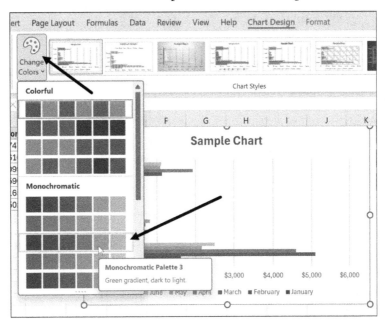

Hold your mouse over each one to see what it will look like. Click to apply.

This is especially useful if you're going to print in black and white. The monochromatic palettes ensure that different chart elements will be easily distinguishable from one another without relying on color difference to make that happen.

Change Chart Colors (Hard Way)

The hard way to change your chart colors is to do so one element at a time using the chart Format tab.

The first step is to click on an element in your chart. Here I've clicked on the blue column that represents April:

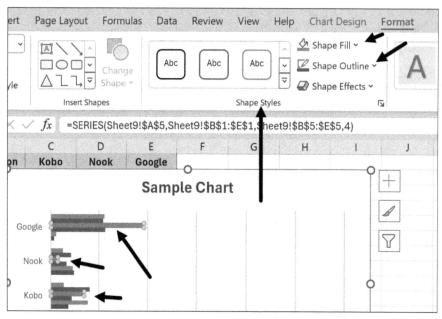

When I clicked on the first April column, Excel selected that column for each store. You may be able to see the dots on each corner for each of those columns. That means all of my April entries will change at the same time. If that doesn't happen, try again.

Once all of a specific element are selected, go to the Shape Styles section of the Format tab.

On the left-hand side are various pre-formatted styles. Click on the downward-pointing arrow with a line behind it to see the full list of options. Hold your mouse over each one to see what it will look like if applied

Here, for example, I have my mouse over a white shape with a colored outline in the first row, and you can see it applied in the chart in the background:

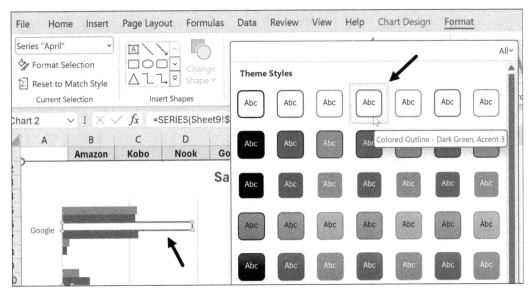

If you don't want to use one of those options, to the right of that are Shape Fill and Shape Outline dropdown options which will let you choose any color you want. (See the image on the last page.)

The More [Fill/Outline] Colors option in those dropdowns will bring up a Color dialogue box where you can choose other colors or input the values for a custom color.

For columns, bars, or pie slices, use the Shape Fill dropdown to choose a main color, and the Shape Outline if you want a different color around the edge.

For lines, use Shape Outline.

Shape Fill also has secondary menus for picture, gradient, and texture, but I would exercise caution in using them. You don't want your formatting to obscure your data.

Outline has secondary menus for line width (weight) and style (dashes).

Hold your mouse over each option to see what it will look like before you click to apply it.

It is possible to combine different fills and outlines for columns, bars, or pie slices like in the pre-formatted example above.

If you customize your colors, just pay attention so that you are keeping the colors distinct for each element. Pay attention to contrast between colors. It is possible to use two different colors that are so similar they might as well be the same, and that pretty much defeats the purpose of having distinct colors for distinct elements.

Change Chart Size

I often need to resize a chart in Excel. One option, if you know the size you want, is to go to the Format tab and enter values for height and width in the Size section:

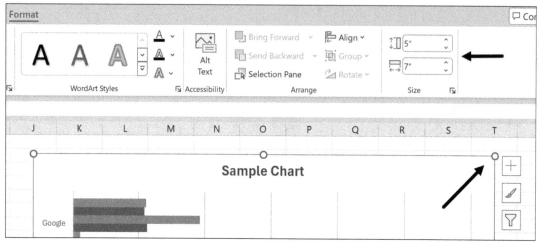

The other option, and the one I use most often, is to click on the chart, and then left-click and drag from one of the white circles around the perimeter. There should be one at each corner as well as one in the middle of each side.

You can see the one in the top right corner of the chart in the image above.

With either option, the size of the various elements in the chart should also adjust.

Chart Styles

Excel provides various pre-formatted styles for each chart type in the Chart Styles section of the Chart Design tab. They contain different colors, layouts, and effects, and will vary depending on the type of chart you chose, as well as any elements you've already added to your chart.

Here, for example, are some options for a column chart:

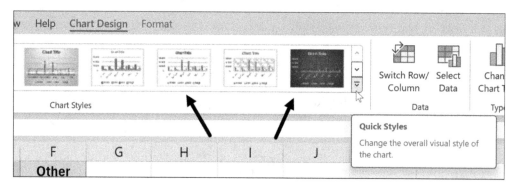

Click on the downpointing arrow with a line behind it in the bottom right corner to see the full set of choices available.

Hold your mouse over each one to see it applied to your chart. Click to keep it.

Personally, I don't think I've ever used any of these, but you should at least look at them once, because they might get you close to an appearance you like.

Quick Layout

Another pre-formatted option can be found in the Quick Layout dropdown menu:

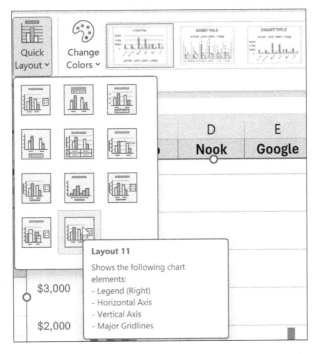

Quick layouts include different chart elements. For example, in the image above I have my cursor over Layout 11. Per Excel that layout would put the legend (that describes my values and their assigned colors) on the right, include a horizontal axis and a vertical axis, and add in major gridlines (which are lines that run across from the side to better help you determine the value that corresponds to a particular column).

Note from the thumbnail image that it would also remove my chart title.

Hold your mouse over each one to see what it will look like applied, click if you want to keep it.

Keep in mind that sometimes a layout will look horrible until you resize your chart to better display all of the elements. (Both here and if you customize your chart yourself.)

Like with chart styles, the quick layouts available will depend on your chart type.

It is possible to apply both a quick layout and a chart style to the same table, since quick layouts are primarily about what chart elements to include, and chart styles are more about the appearance of those elements.

But they do sometimes conflict. Where they conflict, whichever one you selected last will generally be the winner.

If you want to use these, you're just going to have to play around to see what you get.

Add or Modify Chart Element

At the far-left side of the Chart Design tab in the Chart Layouts section is the Add Chart Element dropdown. This is where I go when I want to customize my chart.

Click on the dropdown arrow to see the list of elements you can add or remove. If an element isn't available for a specific type of chart, it will be grayed out like Lines and Up/Down Bars are here:

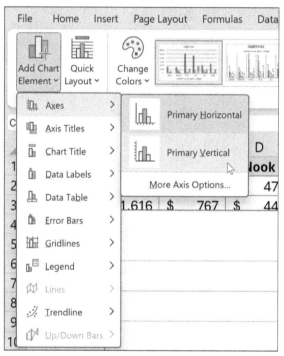

Each element has a secondary dropdown menu, like the one above for Axes, where you can see what choices are available.

Hold your cursor over each option in the secondary dropdown to see what would happen to your chart if you click on it. If the element is already there, clicking on that option will remove it. If it isn't there, then clicking will add or change it to that location.

Keep in mind for text elements that they can sometimes also be manually moved around or resized after you add them.

Now let's walk through each of those choices:

Axes

Your horizontal and vertical axes are what show the values. For a standard chart, horizontal is along the bottom, vertical is along the left side.

If you ever do a combo chart, it's possible to have a secondary vertical axis on the right side and a secondary horizontal axis along the top. The listed options will expand to also let you turn on or off those secondary axes.

Axis Titles

This option lets you add a text box to describe each axis.

Chart Title

This option lets you decide whether to have a chart title and, if you do, whether to put it above the contents of the chart or centered within the chart itself. I personally prefer to have it above, so all the charts in this book have the title in the Above Chart position.

Data Labels

The data labels option lets you decide whether to add the actual values to your chart. For me, I generally only like to do this on pie charts, because I use a data table with most of my bar or column charts that lists the values below the table. It can also get really busy, which makes the chart harder to read.

There are a number of choices about where to place your data labels if you choose to do so. The positions are not fixed.

Here are two options applied to a pie chart, inside end and outside end:

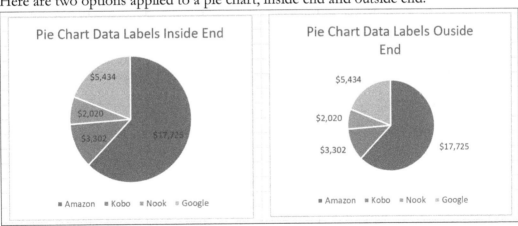

I prefer to have labels on the outside end. (Also, I'll show you how to do this later in the task pane, I tend to prefer to show the % value instead of the dollar value. You can show either one or both.)

You can also click and drag each text box to move them around.

Data Table

The data table option shows the data that created the chart in a table below it. Like here where you can see the dollar values for each store in each month below the columns that represent those values:

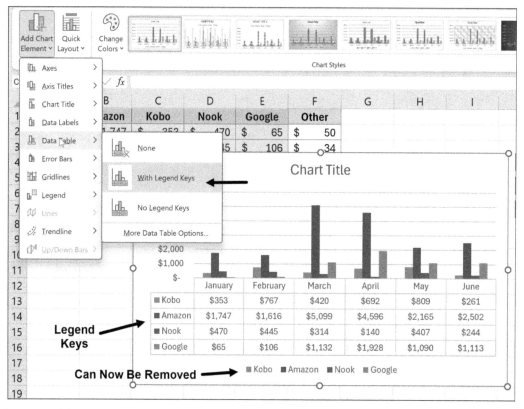

I often use this because I like to have the visual of the chart, but then I also like to see the actual numbers.

You can see that you have a choice to include legend keys or to leave them out. Above I included them. They show the color next to the store name in the data table. The nice thing about doing that is it lets you remove the legend as a separate element.

Error Bars

This option lets you add error bars to the results in your chart. The dropdown contains choices for standard error, percentage, and standard deviation and will apply to all of your category values. For example, with store in the column charts we looked at, you'd have one error bar for each store.

Choosing the More Error Bar Options will let you specify which category values to apply an error bar to. It will also open a Format Error Bars task pane with a custom and a fixed value option. The task pane allows you to control whether the bars go plus, minus, or both, and whether they have a cap at the end.

Gridlines

Gridlines can make it easier to read the data in a chart by providing lines in the background that a reader can follow to the axes to see the associated value.

You can add horizontal or vertical gridlines, and choose to include major lines and/or minor lines. Major lines have wider spacing between each line.

Legend

This option lets you choose where to place the legend (the guide that tells people what color corresponds to what label).

It can be on the top, bottom, left side, or right side. You can also manually position it if you need to as long as you add one.

It is also possible to remove the legend entirely, like I do when I use a data table with legend keys.

Lines

The lines option is available with line and area charts, and allows you to add drop lines and/or high-low lines.

Drop lines draw a vertical line from the top data point down to the horizontal axis.

High-low lines draw a vertical line from the top data point to the bottom data point for each entry.

Trendline

A trendline allows you to add a line onto your chart that either shows a linear or exponential trend based on the values in the chart, shows a linear forecast extrapolated from your values, or shows the moving average of your values.

When you click on this one, it will make you choose one of the values from your legend to create the line from.

The line it inserts will be a dotted line the same color as the category value you chose.

On the next page, for example, I've added trendlines for Amazon and Google:

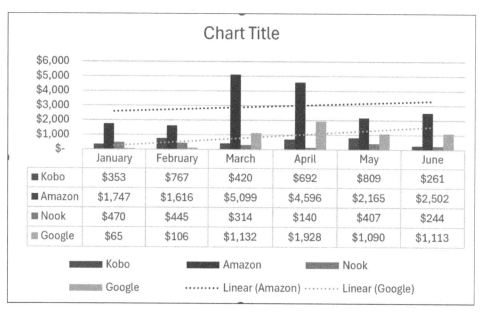

Make sure the type of trendline you choose makes sense for your data. Excel will apply whatever you tell it to, but sometimes the data doesn't justify that. A linear trendline, for example, is not a good choice to use with exponential data.

Up/Down Bars

Up/Down Bars are available for line charts. They draw a bar between two lines on the chart to show a visible change in the distance between the two from entry to entry.

* * *

Format Chart Area Task Pane

As I mentioned above, there is also a task pane option for formatting your chart.

You can open the task pane by double-clicking on your chart. Another option is to right-click on the chart and choose Format Chart Area from the dropdown menu.

You can also choose the More Options choice from any of the secondary dropdown menus for the chart elements.

Using the secondary dropdown menus is probably the best way to get you to the specific task pane you want to work with. You can always navigate there once the task pane is open, by using the dropdowns and icons at the top, but sometimes it's hard to know exactly where to go.

Here, for example, is the task pane that opens when I use the Data Labels secondary dropdown menu for a pie chart to choose More Data Label Options:

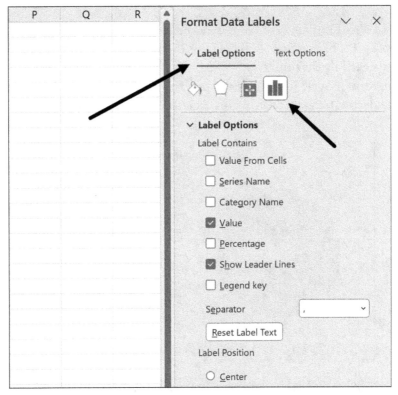

That brought me straight to where I can choose to show data labels as a percent. I could have also added data labels to the pie chart, opened the task pane, changed the top option to Series 1 Data Labels, and then clicked on the fourth icon for Label Options:

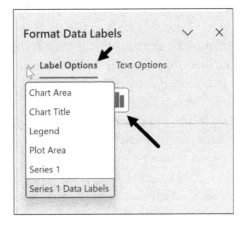

:

(You have to have already added data labels to use that dropdown in the task pane, though.)

Display Pie Chart Percent

The More Data Label Options task pane window (seen above) has a Label Contains section under Label Options. That section has checkboxes for Value, Percentage, and more. For a pie chart, Value is checked by default.

To include percent as well, just check the box for Percentage.

To only include the percent, like in this example, uncheck Value and check the box for Percentage.

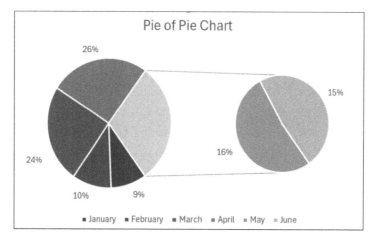

In the above chart I also deleted a box that showed 31% for the pie slice in the main pie chart that is broken out in the secondary chart. (You can do that by just clicking on a text box in the chart and using Delete.)

Leader Lines and Category Name

Two other choices there are Show Leader Lines and Category Name.

Leader lines should be turned on by default even if they aren't initially visible.

I like to have them, because they connect a data label to its element, so even if you have to move data labels around to make everything fit, you can still see what label goes to what element. (Just left-click and drag the text box for a data label to reposition it.)

On the next page, for example, is a pie chart with a lot of values where I had to move the data labels around to keep them from overlapping, and you can see the leader lines that connect each value back to its slice of the pie.

Note the other thing I chose to do here. I turned on Category Name for the data labels, too, so that a legend wasn't needed. With that many slices, trying to distinguish by color just doesn't work well.

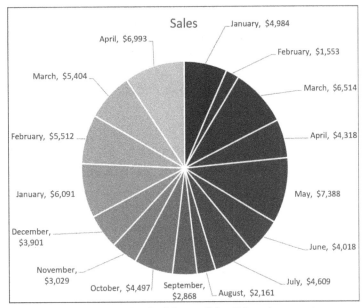

Explode Your Pie Chart

I sometimes like to "explode" a pie chart so that the various slices have space between them. That can be found by clicking on Series Options in the task pane dropdown, and then the third icon listed, which is also Series Options.

(If you can't find one of these settings, try clicking onto that element in your chart and then going to the task pane.)

The higher the percentage you input in the pie explosion box or choose using the slider, the more white space there will be between the various slices of the pie:

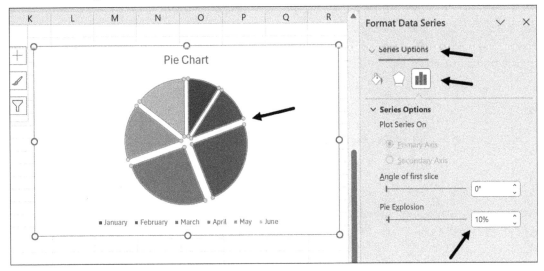

Rotate Your Pie Chart

You can also rotate your pie chart to control which slice is where. To do that, play with the Angle of First Slice setting also located in the Series Options section of the task pane.

Customize Your Histogram

The chart task pane is also the only way I know to customize the size of each histogram bin and the range of values used.

For this one you want Horizontal Axis, Axis Options.

The default is Automatic, but you can specify either the bin width or the number of bins instead.

You can also set the minimum and maximum values using the overflow and underflow bin fields. For example, here I have a range of 10 to 50 with five total bins. Anything under 10 gets dumped into the first bin, anything over 50 gets dumped into the last one. The three in between cover equal ranges of 13.33 each:

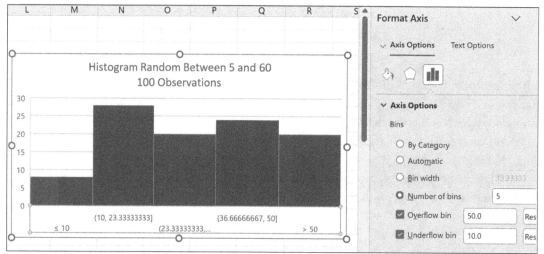

For this one, your chart will update when you click away from the task pane.

* * *

Finally, a few quick points on moving elements or charts around.

Move a Chart

If you need to move the whole chart, left-click and drag. Just be sure not to click on a specific element within the chart or you'll end up moving the element instead. (Remember, Ctrl + Z to Undo.)

You can also select a chart and use Ctrl + X to cut or Ctrl + C to copy, and then go to another worksheet, Word document, or PowerPoint presentation, and use Ctrl + V to paste. (Or your preferred method to copy/cut and paste, I just like the control shortcuts.)

Move or Resize a Chart Element

As I've mentioned a few times already, it is possible to move a chart element around, too. I often move data labels, for example. Just click on that element and drag.

But be aware that sometimes it may not work. I was just struggling to move the chart title on a histogram. I was able to do so just fine on other chart types, but for some reason histograms weren't cooperating with me.

When you click on a chart element that can be edited, there will be white circles at each corner and in the middle of each side that you can left-click and drag to resize. When you resize an element, all of the contents of that element—like the text within a legend—should also resize.

If you don't see white circles, but only blue ones at the corners, you should be able to move that element when your cursor has arrows pointing in four directions by left-clicking and dragging, but you won't be able to resize it.

In general, I don't find I need to manually move or resize elements in charts often. It's more that I accidentally do so sometimes when trying to move the whole chart around. Just remember that Ctrl + Z will undo any mistake you make with a chart.

Pivot Charts

Now that we've finished our discussion of charts, let's circle back to pivot tables, because it is possible to create a chart from data in a pivot table.

The first step is to build the pivot table that has the information you want to use in your chart.

Next, click on your pivot table, and either go to the Tools section of the PivotTable Analyze tab, or to the Charts section of the Insert tab. Both have a PivotChart option.

Click on the PivotChart icon to bring up an Insert Chart dialogue box:

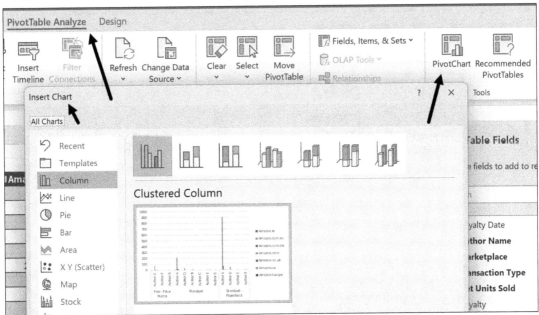

The preview for each chart type will show what your chart will look like given the data in the pivot table. Click on the chart type you want, and then click OK.

The pivot chart that Excel creates will be more dynamic than a standard chart:

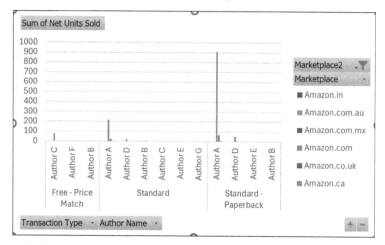

Each of the gray fields that you see in the chart above is a field from the pivot table. The ones that are being used to build the axes—in this case, transaction type, author name, and marketplace (with two levels because I have a group for Amazon Europe)—can be filtered right there in the chart.

Here, for example, I used the Marketplace dropdown and chose to only display results for Amazon Europe:

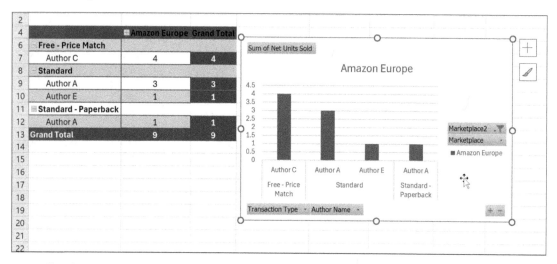

Note what happened to the pivot table in the background when I did that. It automatically updated based on the filters I applied to the chart.

It is important to realize that this connection exists. Because any changes you make to the pivot table will change your pivot chart, and any changes you make to the pivot chart will change your pivot table.

Also, I found that sometimes I needed to go to the pivot chart and update my filters there to see the full data in my pivot table.

If you ever create a pivot chart and you want to "lock it in" so that it can't be impacted by changes you make to the pivot table, you can copy the chart and then paste it special as a picture.

That will lock it in as is. You won't be able to edit it ever.

In terms of formatting your pivot chart, it basically works the same as a normal chart in terms of using the Design and Format tabs or the task pane. Just keep in mind that something like "switch row/column" will also be reflected in your pivot table. It will flip your entries from Rows to Columns and Columns to Rows.

I have found pivot charts particularly useful for things like isolating one value at a time. For example, we've been working with data here that covers different authors or different stores. With a pivot chart, I can use the filter functionality in the chart to quickly show me a chart for each author or each store. Doing that with a standard chart would be much more time-consuming.

Okay. Almost done. Let's cover a few more quick topics and then wrap it up.

Odds and Ends

I always go back and forth on what else people need to know to work in Excel at an intermediate level. For some people, inserting equations or illustrations might be a required skill, but for most people it isn't. Same with inserting symbols. I've devoted chapters to each before in other versions of these books, because sometimes when I'm exploring a new-to-me topic for the first time I like to dive in. But over time that "new information" excitement wears off and I realize no one really cares but me.

So I'm going to do a few topics in this chapter in a fast, high-level way so you know they exist and can go explore them further if they interest you.

Insert Symbols

It is possible that if you're working in Excel, especially if you're using it for text-based analysis, that you will need to insert a symbol at some point. For example, in my day job I have to insert the section symbol that gets used for legal writing. I've also in the past needed the copyright symbol.

There are keyboard shortcuts for these things, so if you use one a lot it may be worth a quick internet search to find the appropriate shortcut to use, but if it's just an occasional thing you need to do, click on the spot in the cell where you need the symbol, and then go to the Symbols section of the Insert tab and click on Symbol.

That will bring up the Symbol dialogue box:

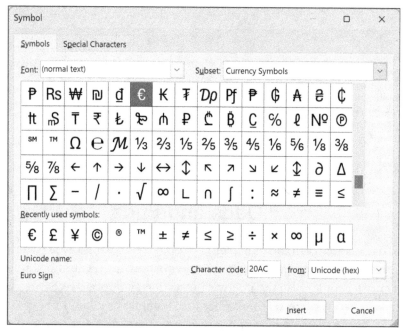

The symbols tab, which is the default, will show your recently used symbols at the bottom, or you can scroll through all of your fonts to find what you need. The dropdowns at the top let you choose a specific font or category of symbol to jump through the list faster. You can also click over to the Special Characters tab to find em dashes, en dashes, copyright, trademark, section, paragraph, etc.

Find the symbol you need, click on it, and then click on Insert.

The dialogue box will remain open. Close it by clicking on the X in the top right corner or Close in the bottom right.

Be careful with inserting symbols and then changing your font. For example, I just inserted a wheel symbol from Wingdings, but when I changed the font it became a right bracket. For common special characters, you're probably fine changing fonts, at least if you use robust ones—it will just change to that font's version of that character—but for more unique shapes or symbols, they can be specific to that particular font.

Once you insert a symbol, you can change the size and color just like any other text.

Insert Equations

In that same section (Symbols section of the Insert tab) is an option for Equation.

If you need to write math in Excel, this is the place to go. The dropdown there has common equations like the area of a circle, binomial theorem, Pythagorean theorem, etc. Click on one of those choices to insert a text box on top of your worksheet.

When you have an equation like this inserted onto your worksheet, and you are clicked onto it, there will be an Equation tab available that has a zillion components you can use to build an equation, as well as common structures you can insert, like fractions:

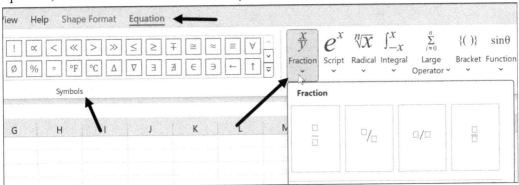

Click on an element to add it to your equation. If there are boxes, like with the fraction examples above, click on each box and then either type a value or click on another element to complete the box.

There is an option to "ink an equation" that lets you write the equation yourself with a stylus.

There are also three formats you can use for your equations depending on the notation style you prefer.

Insert Illustrations

You can also insert pictures, shapes, icons, 3D models, SmartArt, and screenshots in Excel. These options are found in the Illustrations section of the Insert tab. Most will insert on top of the worksheet, not in a particular cell.

You can change their size, color, etc. once inserted.

If you have more than one, you can control which one displays in the forefront or background when they overlap by using the Arrange section of the menu tab for that type of illustration.

Quick Access Toolbar

If you ever find yourself moving back and forth between two different tabs a lot, because you're using different tasks that are located in different tabs, it may be possible to add one or the other of them to the Quick Access Toolbar. This will make that task always available in the top left corner of your workspace.

To add another task to the Quick Access Toolbar, click on the downward-pointing arrow with a line at the end of your currently available tasks:

You can see that it says Customize Quick Access Toolbar in the image above when I hold my mouse over it. And that I currently have save, undo, redo, and format painter available.

When you click on that arrow, it will bring up a dropdown menu of popular options. Ones with a check next to them are displayed in the quick access toolbar, ones without a check are not. If you see the one you want, click on it to put a check next to it. If you don't see the option you want, click on More Commands.

That will open a dialogue box with all possible choices:

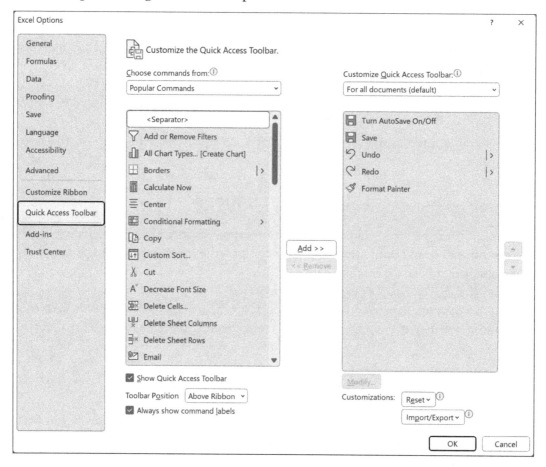

To add a task, find it on the left-hand side, click on it, and then click Add in the center. To remove a task, find it on the right-hand side, click on it, and then click on Remove in the center.

Excel Options

You may have noticed that the dialogue box above was called Excel Options, and that Quick Access Toolbar was just one of a number of options listed along the side.

That's because you can also open this dialogue box by going to the File tab and then clicking on Options in the bottom left corner. Excel Options lets you do a lot of different things to customize your Excel experience. I'd say it's worth exploring if there is anything Excel regularly does that annoys you or that you have to undo.

For example, I normally change the default save location. They love to save to OneDrive and I just want to save to my C drive.

I also tend to turn off certain error corrections, like turning (c) into the copyright symbol since I am more likely to be citing a rule. And I prefer to set my privacy settings to not access the internet or whatever it is they have going on with LinkedIn.

I would caution against getting too fancy with customizing your Excel options, though, because you still want to be able to use someone else's version of Excel when needed.

Zoom

It is possible to zoom in or out to increase or decrease the size of the cells in your worksheet and make their contents more or less visible.

If you ever need to do this, the easiest option is in the bottom right corner. There is a line there with a minus at one end, a plus sign at the other end, a percentage displayed for the current zoom level, and a perpendicular bar somewhere along the line

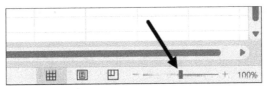

The perpendicular bar marks where you currently are. Click to the left of that bar to make things smaller, click to the right to make them bigger. You can also click and drag the bar.

Your other option is to go to the Zoom section of the View tab:

The 100% option there will take your view back to a 100% zoom level.

Clicking on the Zoom option will open a dialogue box with options for 200%, 100%, 75%, 50%, 25%, Fit Selection, or Custom.

Zoom to selection will zoom to show all of the selected cells. (Even if you select a lot of them, so be careful there.)

Note that zoom only affects the cells in your worksheet, not the menu up top, task panes, or dialogue boxes. You need to maximize Excel to take up your entire screen, use a bigger monitor, or change your Windows settings to get any of those to be larger.

Hide a Worksheet

If you ever need to hide a worksheet, right-click on its name and choose Hide from the dropdown menu.

Other worksheets will still be able to reference that one, but users won't be able to see it unless they unhide it. This can come in handy if you ever need to reference a list of values that don't need to be visible to users.

Unhide a Worksheet

To unhide a worksheet, right-click on a currently visible worksheet, and then choose Unhide from the dropdown menu. This will bring up an Unhide dialogue box that will list all hidden worksheets in that workbook. Click on the one(s) you want and then click on OK.

Navigate a Large Number of Worksheets

If you have a large number of worksheets in a workbook, right-click on the arrows at the left bottom end that you use to navigate between worksheets to bring up the Activate dialogue box:

You can then click on the worksheet you want, and click OK to move to it.

Indent Text within a Cell

If you ever want to indent text or values within a cell, use the Increase Indent option that's located in the bottom row of the Alignment section of the Home tab. It has lines with a right-pointing arrow. You can indent more than once.

I've used this when I had a summary row above detailed rows of data and wanted to create a visual break between the two.

To remove an indent, use the Decrease Indent option which has the left-pointing arrow. If you indented more than once, you will need to decrease the indent more than once also.

The Format Cells dialogue box also has an Indent field in the Alignment tab that will let you specify the number of times to indent the text in the selected cell(s).

Notes in Excel

If you're using a worksheet that someone else created and you see a red mark in the top right corner of a cell, especially in a header row, it is possible that there are instructions or further explanation available for that field. Hold your cursor over that cell to see the comment:

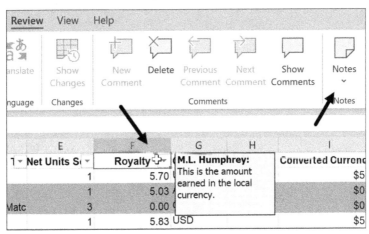

To add a note yourself, click on the cell, go to the Review tab, and use the dropdown under Notes in the Notes section. Select New Note and then type what you want in the note field that appears. You can also use the Notes dropdown to edit an existing note or move between the notes in a worksheet.

The show notes options available there will make notes visible by default.

Conclusion

Okay. That's all we're going to cover in this book. We're just over thirty thousand words which is pretty much the upper limit for one of these books. Past that point I think we cross the line from something a person can read cover to cover to a resource that only gets used for learning specific topics.

The next book in this series is going to dive in on the last big topic I want to cover with respect to Excel, which is how formulas and functions work. It covers about seventy total functions with fifty having their own chapter.

So what didn't I cover here that you may still need to know?

I didn't cover how to lock a workbook or cells from being edited. It's just not one I've had to use often. Same with the different workbook views or accessibility.

And there are definitely some very big more advanced topics out there like macros or PowerBi. There are plenty of books on those topics by people far better at using them than I am. Using them is like learning a computer programming language. Not for the faint of heart.

As a reminder, you can always go to the Help tab to search for how to do different things in Excel. There are also a zillion resources out there, and the Microsoft support website is great.

You can also reach out to me and I'll try to help, too, especially if something in here wasn't clear. Or if I got it wrong. I try to test everything I write in these books, but I am not perfect. Sometimes I test something and it works one way and that's how I describe it, and then later I happen to do it a little differently and it turns out there was a bit of nuance there that I'd missed the first time around.

This is the fourth series of these books I've written, so hopefully I've caught most of those issues by now, but I always find something the next time around.

And they do change Excel on a regular basis. Usually on the fringes, thankfully, but sometimes in more core areas. I think I mentioned that I've noticed that filtering is now a little wonky in Excel 365. The good news about working in Excel 2024 instead of Excel 365 is that it will remain stable for you as long as you use it. (Theoretically. I think sometimes they try to get in there and update things even on the stable versions.)

Anyway.

Good luck with it. You can do this. It's a lot to take in when you're just getting started, but remember that under all of this there is a certain logic. If you get stuck or confused, try to think about how something similar works in Excel, and then take that approach.

Also, remember that Ctrl + Z, Undo, is your friend. It will get you out of a lot of mistakes. And Esc is often a good way to just shut things down and back away.

Okay then. If you're ready to keep going, check out the next book in the series, *Excel 2024 Useful Functions.*

Index

About the Author

M.L. Humphrey is a former stockbroker with a degree in Economics from Stanford and an MBA from Wharton who has spent close to twenty-five years as a regulator and consultant in the financial services industry.

You can reach M.L. at mlhumphreywriter@gmail.com or at mlhumphrey.com.

If you want to buy this book as an ebook, use code EXCEL2024 at https://payhip.com/mlhumphrey to get a fifty percent discount.